NAMING *and* TAMING *Overwhelm*

For Healthcare and Human Service Providers

BY SARRI GILMAN, LMFT

Sarri Gilman

Naming and Taming Overwhelm / By Sarri Gilman
ISBN: 978-0-9897787-4-9
First Printing, 2017

Published by Healthy Gen Media,
a division of Foundation for Healthy Generations
and Island Bound Publishing

Book layout and design by Tarsha Rockowitz

Dedication

For Melanie Gillespie and the Foundation for Healthy Generations, who believed in this book and provided support to write it.

For my colleagues in the field, who have dedicated their lives to serving others and faced many overwhelming things. I have watched you closely and distilled from your effective strategies and my own the things I believe make a difference.

For my daughters, who entered the field of healthcare: Somer Kreisman, DPT, Aliza Kreisman, DNP-FNP BSN-RN, and Saralyn Kortlever, RN.

For Sally Landsburg, who helped me find my calling and sent me on my path. May these words honor you.

For my clients, you illuminated my understanding during the past three decades. Your strength and commitment to therapy and your willingness to face the Overwhelm has often left me in awe. I am only able to share this because you have shown me what helps.

Acknowledgements

I am grateful for all the support I received to write this book. Deborah Nedelman, Ph.D, has served as my book midwife, discussing the concepts, the writing, to make the book a better book. She was also the book midwife for my previous book, *Transform Your Boundaries*. She is a retired therapist and a writing coach, and she asks me questions as I write, questions that help me find my way.

Melanie Gillespie and the Foundation for Healthy Generations believed in the idea of this book early on and provided publishing support for this book. Melanie is a leader and a capacity builder in our field. Very few people have her unique blend of gifts, and we are fortunate she has spent her career in our field. I am fortunate that we worked together in the past and reconnected. The Foundation for Healthy Generations will be making this material highly accessible to people who work in healthcare and human services.

My husband Ken, for feeding my body and soul, becoming an outstanding cook during the writing of this book. He is also a project manager and has figured out how to give me exactly what I need to keep writing. Many writers need to get away to write; I need to be home.

Ben and Candice Kortlever, for their love, support and kindness.

My deepest gratitude to the organizations that have been using my work, *Transform Your Boundaries*. I hope this book is helpful and supports you in your good work.

There are a couple of people behind the scenes who have become very involved in helping my work reach people. My deepest thanks to Erika Olson, Brian Houck, Sno-Isle Libraries, Jonalyn Woolf-Ivory, Ken Harvey, Phil Klein, Kathy Coffey, Norma Jean Straw, Tarsha Rockowitz, Carol Snider, Bennie Soto, Omid Bagheri, Valerie Landsburg, Lon Haber, Tammy Green, Adrianne Wagner, Charlene Ray, Robin Barre, and Kathy Burgoyne, who found a home for this book immediately.

This book is based on my observations, experiences, and questions. There has been plenty of research by others that has informed and confirmed my perspective.

This book would not and could not exist without all of the trauma researchers and teachers who have passed along effective strategies for dealing with trauma. Our clinical understanding of trauma has changed and evolved over the years, and it is a field that is continuing to grow. I have been a student of trauma for the past thirty years.

Though the topic of overwhelm may include trauma, I have seen many people experience overwhelm who were not concurrently traumatized. But I believe my understanding of trauma allowed me to ask how overwhelm was similar and different from trauma. My deepest gratitude to the many trauma researchers around the globe and who over time contributed so much to my understanding.

Foreword

If you've picked up this book, we might have something in common. Let me tell you, you've come to the right place. Sarri Gilman is the real deal, and *Naming and Taming Overwhelm* is the book we all need.

We live in interesting times. Information is coming at us at a rate never seen before in history. Our brains are not wired for this. For those of us with a passion and a dedication to helping others, the overwhelm can get intense as we see more and more clients, our patients, and our community members living under increasingly stressful situations. A pileup of research tells us the damage toxic stress can do to our bodies and our opportunities for whole, healthy lives.

Meanwhile, the organizations within which we work or with whom we interface are also increasingly overwhelmed. Budget problems are causing cutbacks. Caseloads are going up. Everyone is expected to "do more with less" at "optimal efficiency." Administrators and managers in health and human service systems are also experiencing the stress of overwhelmed systems.

I've known Sarri for about twenty years. When I first met her, she was in the midst of work that was causing her great stress and overwhelm. It was great work. Important work. Saving lives of young people on a daily basis. This work was started from a place of personal calling and devotion to making the world a better place. Does this sound familiar? It should. This book is written for all of us who are called to help others.

That calling to help others comes from deep in our spirit and brings us great joy and profound meaning. As we understand more from research these days, having meaningful activities in our lives is literally good for our health. Giving to others is literally good for our health. This is possibly the ultimate example of enlightened self-interest. And, yet...

Too many of us have found ourselves and our organizations mired in overwhelm. Overwhelm feels like a Paleolithic era tar pit. We get stuck in it and suddenly, the more we struggle and flail, using the same action that got us there in the first place, the more we sink and get stuck. Until we feel we can't breathe. And maybe we literally can't, as overwhelm can tip some of us into severe anxiety and panic. This is overwhelm. Sarri is here to help you get out of that tar pit.

Sarri's path has brought her into close contact with overwhelm in both her personal life and her professional life.

She knows what's she's talking about based on deep intimacy as well as strong, relevant professional and clinical training. This is a potent brew.

Talking with Sarri while she was writing this book got me so excited about what is being shared with you now. Sarri has distilled down her thirty years of experience as a visionary leader, a licensed counselor, a practiced trainer, and a highly acclaimed author into this book. When I first read the manuscript, I was impressed by the way she had compressed every idea and offering into the most simple and most economical use of words possible. That's hard to do!

Every word in this book counts. Sarri hasn't burdened us with any extra words. She doesn't want her book to overwhelm you. It's not another "should" or "to do." (Oh, you have those lists too? Happy to meet you, friend...) She takes our hand on page one and says (in my mind), "Come with me. I know the way through this maze of overwhelm. We'll go together, and we'll rest as often as you need along the way." I cried more than once reading this book. Sometimes I cried because a learning hit a personal nerve, but I cried just as often at the boundless love and deep caring I could feel on every page.

I had the opportunity seventeen years ago to work with Sarri for a period. She had asked me to come in and help her organization. She was in overwhelm and so was the agency. Sarri is a powerful force of nature, and she had grown a small emergency shelter for homeless youth into a significant enterprise. Managing this complex entity wasn't something she had the calling or the training to do. She figured out how to get help, and one of those forms of help was me.

But let me be clear: I was the one who got the better of the deal. As we worked in partnership to help her agency catch up with the current demands and provide needed systems for her team, Sarri was also teaching me about how to value myself and what I uniquely bring to the table. She was very firm about it. Okay, she was actually very pushy about it! (She's laughing right now as she reads this). I learned lessons from that time that remain valuable and relevant to me today.

For all these reasons and more, it is such a gift to have the Foundation for Healthy Generations partnering with Sarri to bring needed resources and tools to help people "stay well while doing good." At Healthy Gen, our mission is to create enduring health equity. We believe that people and communities thrive when all are healthy, included, and connected. Health equity work is hard. It's a long game. Healthy Gen's role is to be a catalyst to support the actions of the many people across many disciplines and in many communities who are needed to do the work of shifting our way of thinking from "me to we" so that all can have the same opportunity to have a healthy, whole life.

In our role as the "help that helps" to the helpers (that would be you!), we bring many resources to bear. One such resource is philanthropic giving, including "attention philanthropy," in which we use our resources to spotlight great things that are happening, especially those things that might otherwise go unnoticed in the crazy hubbub of our current time. We also support public/private coalitions doing the real work with a commitment to a system of community engagement. We have refined this system to create authentic connection and illuminate more clearly the meaning of key health and social determinant data. In addition, we provide a variety of free trainings and resources and do our best to show up as people whenever we can and wherever it seems most useful.

This work is not for the faint of heart. We know that. You know that. We're committed to that and so are you. But that doesn't mean we don't get mired in overwhelm too, no matter how good we are at this work. It may even be true that the better you are at it, the more at risk for overwhelm you will find yourself. I don't believe anyone currently living in this country is immune to overwhelm. We need practical, tactical tools to help us when we get overwhelmed, to get our life preservers back on, and to be able to keep our chin up above the waterline.

In hope research, the key points defining hope are: 1) the ability to imagine a goal for yourself; 2) the ability to visualize the pathways to get you there; and 3) the sense of wherewithal in yourself that you can do it. Clinically, one might call it "agency" or "self-efficacy." I call it moxie, gumption, spirit, badassery in general. I've had the privilege of knowing a hope researcher named Dr. Chan Hellman, and he taught me, among many things, that "hope is a social gift" because we are each other's pathways. *Naming and Taming Overwhelm* is just such a pathway. Take hope into your heart because you have a key in your hand right now. A key to unlock your life and those of the people you work with such that all can return to the joy and passion that got us here in the first place.

Thank you for all you do. You do it every day. Maybe take a few days off now and then, come to think of it! You are making a better world. Don't forget to make sure it's better for you too. We love you at Healthy Gen. Think of this book and related tools as our love letter to you. Take a breath. Grab a cup of tea. Find a cozy nook with a snuggly blanket and open this book. You might want a pen handy to jot down your thoughts as they bubble up or write in the margins. I did. It's not going anywhere.

You are not on a timer for this. Give yourself the gift of open time to read just the right amount for you at a time. Come back later and read a bit more. Or maybe, like me, you'll come back later and reread a compelling section. Share what you learn with others. Just like you already do. Everyday.

Love,

Melanie

Melanie Gillespie
Executive Director
Foundation for Healthy Generations
Seattle, Washington
March 2017

Preface

Take your time to read. You work with overwhelm, see it, live it. Reading about it is not intended to overwhelm you further. I have written with that in mind, but going slowly through the book may be helpful. Also, please read the sections and chapters in the order presented because I introduce concepts and reference them in later chapters.

This book is divided into three parts:

- Part I. Working with Clients Who Are Overwhelmed

- Part II. Getting a Life Jacket on You, the Provider

- Part III. Widespread Overwhelm, the Overwhelm around You

The stories I have written about myself in this book are true. To protect the privacy of people I have known, no real names or personal, private, confidential stories from other people are used in this book. None of the individuals you are reading about are actual people. They are composites created to give you tangible examples.

The stories will ring true, however, because if you work with people who are overwhelmed, you have seen and heard stories just like these.

Table of Contents

Part I: Working With Clients Who Are Overwhelmed

Chapter One: What Is Overwhelm

- Story about Devi and Dan

- Story about JC

- Defining overwhelm

Chapter Two: How Do You Treat Overwhelm

- Get a life jacket on the client

- Listen

- Stop problem solving

- Be a spider

- Discuss boundaries

Part II: Getting a Life Jacket on You, the Provider

Chapter Three: What Is Provider Overwhelm

- Story about Mira

- Overwhelm spreads

- Caring for your feelings

Chapter Four: Protecting Yourself from Overwhelm

- Dealing with the gray cloud

- Strategies for understanding your feelings

- What if it doesn't help

Chapter Five: The Need for Supervision and Mentoring

- Supervision for supervisees

- Supervision for supervisors

Chapter Six: Protecting Your Boundaries

- Defining your time

- Defining your job

- Defining your role

Chapter Seven: Healthy Supports for the Helpers

Part III: Widespread Overwhelm, the Overwhelm around You

Chapter Eight: What Is Community Overwhelm

- Story about Manny

- Defining community overwhelm

Introduction

The year that I wrote this book marked my thirty years in the field of healthcare and human services. This thirtieth year was a significant marker for me, and as I reflected back, I was also thinking forward about our field and the next thirty years.

I have had a profoundly satisfying career in healthcare and human services. It has been challenging, meaningful, joyful, and painful. Not always one or the other, but a mix of feelings from witnessing deeply the lives of others. The joy and passion I have had for working closely with people during thirty years has never left me. I love what I do each day. Working with others has transformed me, and I have taken notes on what I have learned along the way.

For me, this book is a small lighthouse, blinking in the night. I hope this book lights the rocky shore for those of you serving now and in the future. Feeling overwhelm, treating overwhelm, and preventing or recovering from your own overwhelm is the rocky shore.

There are many skills you develop to thrive and be effective in this field. Whatever your particular job is in this field, "soft skills" are emphasized at least somewhat, and there are many checkpoints for assessing these skills. I agree that while mastering soft skills is essential, I have found that there are two other skills that are equally important. Neither of these issues has received the attention or emphasis it deserves. There is so much to learn to do our kind of work, and it's easy to skip over or miss the two other skills that will sustain you in your career. These skills are buried under a sea of other things competing for your attention. It may be hard to recognize their significance and how much these two things support our field. The two skills are:

- managing boundaries
- understanding and treating overwhelm

In my first book, *Transform Your Boundaries*, I spelled out a very clear map for building healthy boundaries. I wrote that book for a general audience; anyone can relate to it, as I have learned from readers around the globe. But people in healthcare, human services, and education found the book really spoke to them. I created a workshop to accompany the book and help people understand boundaries through their life stories. I created and continue to teach workshops and online classes about healthy boundaries specifically for healthcare and human service providers. In a TEDx talk called "Good

Boundaries Free You," I shared my own journey recovering my boundaries and the need for self-care when working in our field.

The feedback and messages I have received about the benefits of *Transform Your Boundaries*, the TEDx talk, and my workshops have led me to write the book you are now holding in your hands. People who work in the field of education will also find this book relatable. They too are exposed to overwhelm and will benefit from this book.

It is very clear to me that "overwhelm" is on the rise. Right now and in the near future, people need essential tools and help when they are in overwhelming circumstances. Is our field of helping professionals in the broad category of healthcare and human services prepared to handle these increasingly overwhelming circumstances, or are we also overwhelmed ourselves? Notice how often you hear someone say, "I am overwhelmed." Notice how often you feel overwhelmed.

I hope when you are finished with this book, or even as you are reading, you will improve caring for yourself and will encourage your coworkers to take overwhelm seriously and take steps to address it. Those of us who work in health and human services are not more resilient than other people. We are all vulnerable to overwhelm. We need language to talk about it and ways to support each other and those who come to us as clients or patients. (For simplicity, I will be using the word "client" rather than "patient" throughout the book.)

This book is divided into sections and stories. The stories may be challenging to read, as some of you working in the field may feel it is too much to take in one more story. It is okay to skip the stories if they are too hard to read. It is okay to read at the pace that works for you. Go slowly. Take it in bit by bit. I have tried to keep space on the page and research to a minimum, and to not make the book an overwhelming text to read.

I honor your intelligence, your experience, and the work you are doing in the field. While you read this book, you may be working with clients where you noticed and felt their overwhelm. You may feel overwhelmed right now by working with too many clients. You may be working in an organization or institution that is overwhelmed. You may have a supervisor who is overwhelmed. You may be experiencing change in your field that is moving at a pace that you feel you can't keep up with. You may feel like you cannot catch your breath or get free from thinking about it during your time off.

My hope is that you will make decisions about the boundaries that you, your clients, and organizations in your field need to be healthy. Sometimes we are standing with our ear to an ocean of overwhelm, listening. This book explores the question of how to stand in an ocean of overwhelm without becoming overwhelmed.

PART I:

Working with Clients Who Are Overwhelmed

Notes:

_____

_____

_____

_____

_____

_____

_____

_____

_____

_____

_____

_____

_____

_____

_____

_____

CHAPTER ONE:

What Is Overwhelm

Story about Devi and Dan

Dan, age twenty-seven, is part of a film crew making a low-budget video in South America. While filming in a remote area, he becomes very sick. When he seems to be getting worse, he is taken to the nearest hospital. Seven days later, as Dan seems to be recovering, the film crew moves on to their next remote location in Africa, leaving Dan with an open airline ticket to return to the United States.

Devi, Dan's fiancée, calls and talks with him each day in the hospital, but on the fourth day, she can't reach him. When she checks with the hospital, she is told he is in a coma. The hospital explains that they have been unable to stop the progress of the unknown virus. They aren't sure what the virus is, but Dan is in a coma.

Dan's closest living relative is his eighteen-year-old brother Elliot. Dan's parents are deceased: one has passed away from cancer and the other from a heart attack. Elliot is in his freshman year of college.

Devi contacts Elliot. Elliot is not sure what he is supposed to do. Dan is the older brother and has always figured things out for both of them. Elliot wants to help, but he isn't sure what kind of help he needs to get for Dan. He asks a million questions that Devi does not know the answers to.

Devi tries to arrange a way to fly Dan to a hospital in the United States, but because of his virus, Dan is not allowed to enter the United States. Instead, comatose Dan is airlifted to a hospital in Paris, France.

Devi, who has very little money, calls friends asking for financial help to get to Paris. Elliot does not want to be left behind, and Devi isn't sure she can sign any papers or make any decisions without Elliot. She realizes she needs to raise more money to take Elliot. Devi worries about Elliot losing his college scholarship by missing classes. She worries that Dan would not want Elliot to lose his college opportunity.

Devi has recently been in a car accident and is suffering from a concussion. She has painful headaches, has trouble making decisions, and cries from distress each day.

When you meet with Devi, she cries as she tries to explain what has happened. There are times when she is sobbing and can't catch her breath.

Think about this situation:

- What would you ask Devi to learn more about her situation and assess her needs?

- From your particular field, what resources could you recommend for Devi, Dan, or Elliot?

- Who could you call in your personal or professional network to find out about resources?

- Where would you reach out to or suggest Devi turn to?

- Is there something you could offer Devi in the way of checking in with her to be part of her circle of support? You may not be a big part of her support, but what can you offer to show concern and be of some support to Devi?

Story about JC

JC has been diagnosed with breast cancer. Her employer is laying off hundreds of people in the upcoming month. JC goes to her employer and explains that she has been diagnosed with breast cancer and cannot afford to lose her health insurance. Her employer figures out a way to keep her employed for an extra sixty days, but after that, JC is laid off.

She cannot afford to keep her health insurance, so she immediately enrolls in the state health insurance program. Her new insurance program insists that her care be transferred to a different hospital and new oncologist. The new oncologist cannot get approval from the insurance provider for the cancer treatment protocol JC has been given.

The new options presented to JC involve surgery and discontinuing her medication. Her medications will run out in twenty days. JC calls different providers and tries to find a care team that can continue her current protocol and accept her insurance.

Still unemployed, JC begins to search for a new job to keep her unemployment support. Her unemployment check is not enough to cover her apartment, food, and bills. JC tells her employment counselor that she is so stressed, she can't sleep.

Think about this situation:

- How are you feeling as you read this story?

- Do you know anyone who has gone through cancer treatment?

- What sort of ideas come to mind to help JC?

- What kind of help do you think she needs?

- What questions would you ask JC?

- What kinds of resources are available in the work you do to help JC? What can you offer?

- How would you be affected if you were working with multiple clients like this?

Defining overwhelm

I wish this was a feeling I had recognized and understood thirty years ago. I think there were many times when I had witnessed something that was overwhelming or felt overwhelmed myself but did not realize I was overwhelmed. I was working with an overwhelmed system, seeing overwhelmed people, and feeling at times overwhelmed myself.

One day, I was sitting on the exam table in my doctor's office. He stepped out of the exam room and left my chart on the table. (This was when medical charts were handwritten and kept in folders.) I picked up my medical chart and read that I was "exhausted." True. I flipped to the next page, "exhausted." Next page, "exhausted." As I flipped through the two-inch stack of pages, I lost count of how many times that word appeared in my medical record over a ten-year period. I remember feeling this sense that there was something underlying this exhaustion, something deeper, and I didn't have words for it.

But now knowing what I know, I realize what appeared as exhaustion was actually overwhelm. But the word wasn't common then. The feelings were there, the experience certainly, but there wasn't really a word for it. I didn't know what "it" was.

I was treated for "exhaustion" and told to rest. My doctor and I repeated this cycle over and over throughout a decade.

Eventually, I became curious about and interested in my own workaholism, self-care, and boundaries. I realized there was a way to respond to overwhelm that was incredibly helpful. Rest is a great cure for exhaustion, but recognizing and dealing with overwhelm helped me recover and heal from a repeated cycle. Of course, if I only had myself as a study case, I would not be writing this book. I became very aware of people who were overwhelmed. I realized I was treating many people who were overwhelmed and working with colleagues who were overwhelmed.

After 2008, I noticed a shift in people. The word overwhelm was used more and more. It became a way to describe yourself. Now, people say they are overwhelmed. When I ask what is going on, I hear a list of things that is profoundly overwhelming. As a therapist, I began to focus on that word, how people were using it, what it meant to them. I began to see pieces of a puzzle come together. There was something deep, true, and diagnostic about the word "overwhelm." It named something that was everywhere, surrounding us, inside of us, needing to be recognized and understood.

As a psychotherapist, I find the word and feeling of overwhelm extremely important. Though the word isn't in our diagnostic manuals or a service list, I believe it is an indicator word. When a red light goes on in your car, it is an indicator. When someone says they are overwhelmed, it is a red blinking indicator. Stop and figure out why the light is red. Pay attention when someone says they are overwhelmed.

When someone uses the word "suicidal" in healthcare and human services, everyone's head turns, a whole of bunch of responsive interactions occur. That word means something in every health and human service system. I believe the word "overwhelm" is as important as the word "suicidal." Every person working in healthcare and human services needs to be able to recognize overwhelm and know what they can do when someone is in a state of overwhelm.

A few years ago, I started defining overwhelm as a state of "too muchness." We are all suffering from having too much to do, too many expectations, too many unsolvable problems, too many issues at home. The amount of things we are trying to deal with is part of the definition. But overwhelm is more than too muchness. The definition needs to include the way that overwhelm impacts a person.

Overwhelm is pervasive stress on the body and mind, deeply affecting your problem-solving abilities.

Overwhelm is invasive. It is as if you are hijacked by a situation or several situations at once. You can't address the overload by yourself, but you may not realize this fact. It can't possibly be managed by one person. Because there is "too much" and it is "too invasive" in your body and mind, you are stretched too thin and beyond your capacity.

People who are great problem solvers, people you work with in health and human services, will have trouble solving problems when they are overwhelmed.

In JC's story, she is overwhelmed by her circumstances. An additional fact is that her employment counselor and doctor also find JC's situation overwhelming. The employment counselor is working with JC on resume writing, preparing for interviews, and all the while JC is teary and can't stop crying.

The doctor is writing letters, making phone calls, and trying to get the insurance company to continue the original treatment plan. But the doctor is worried because JC lives alone, is sick, and is under pressure to find a new job. The doctor is spending lots of extra time on JC's case but doesn't have anything to show for it in terms of getting JC what she needs medically.

When you hear your client describe a very challenging situation, you may find yourself unsure about what would be helpful. You may get overwhelmed thinking about it. It is important to remember that, no matter how many times you see overwhelmed clients during the day, overwhelm is not a "normal" state of being. If you see it often, you may forget. If everyone around you, your peers, or colleagues seems overwhelmed, you may think it is just part of the job.

We can't avoid or ignore how it is impacting our field, our coworkers, our clients, and ourselves.

Overwhelm indicates a high level of internal stress. The stress we experience in our bodies from overwhelm—the tension, anxiety, and depletion—is not good for our mental or physical health. We also can't pretend it will go away. It is not going away. We are not going to "adjust" to it and just consider it the new normal. There are consequences for being overwhelmed: mistakes, accidents, illness, high-employee turnover, personal relationship erosion, depression, poor problem solving, exhaustion, numbing and, ultimately, perpetuation of overwhelm. I promise the list of consequences is much longer. And if we don't do something about it, it will undermine our effectiveness.

In healthcare and human services, we treat or respond based on what we recognize. We label or diagnosis what is happening. We start by naming, recognizing what is happening. This is why it is so important to recognize and define overwhelm.

Whatever role you play in healthcare or human services, when you see a JC, you need to know her whole situation. You can't just slice off one piece of her life and treat that. Everything you do with JC to help, treat, or support her must take into consideration the fact that she is overwhelmed. You will be more effective if your strategies are shaped by that knowledge. How you relate to JC will make more sense if you have an understanding of how overwhelm affects her.

A client can be overwhelmed by things happening around them. These may include problems with a water system in a town, an overwhelming job, a family member, racism in a community, financial issues. No matter where the overwhelming situations are happening, people have an internal response.

Overwhelm can touch every aspect of a person's life.

Overwhelm is different than being "needy." People who seem "needy" are often wanting your attention and are capable of doing more to care for themselves than they may be doing. When you are with someone who is needy, notice how you feel. You may feel annoyed. You are probably thinking, "They should be able to solve this issue on their own; they are attention seeking."

When you are with someone who is overwhelmed, you are probably feeling worried about the person. You are thinking, "This is an overwhelming situation."

No one is immune to overwhelm. It can happen to anyone.

Overwhelm can happen at any age, any education level, any income level. Highly capable people can become overwhelmed given the right set of circumstances. I have worked with doctors, lawyers, nurse practitioners, and business owners who have suffered from overwhelm. I also worked with teens and families who were homeless, also suffering from overwhelm. I have worked with frontline staff and executives in healthcare, human services, and education. All, at points, suffered from overwhelm.

Defining overwhelm is key to treating your clients when they are overwhelmed. Your client may not recognize it or have the word for it. In addition, your effectiveness will greatly increase if you are able to acknowledge that your client is overwhelmed. There is a difference between simply recognizing overwhelm and acknowledging it. When you acknowledge it, you are letting your client know that you see they are overwhelmed.

I have introduced you to some of the core components of how I define overwhelm. For me it can include: too many things to manage at once; a pervasive stress on the body and mind; difficulty problem solving; and problems that may be unsolvable.

You work with people. I want you to create your definition. Use the time and space you need to write your definition. As you go through this book, you can refine your definition.

Take time to reflect:

- What are your thoughts on overwhelm?

- What do you think it is?

- How do you recognize it?

Notes:

_____

_____

_____

_____

_____

_____

_____

_____

_____

_____

_____

CHAPTER TWO:

How Do You Treat Overwhelm

Get a life jacket on the client

Now that you have a definition and way to recognize overwhelm, how do you respond to someone who is overwhelmed? There is not a "one size fits all" approach for overwhelm. While there are well-researched programs to reduce stress or deal with trauma, these programs aren't necessarily a fit for every person who is overwhelmed. Sending people into a meditation program or mindfulness program may be very helpful. However, treating overwhelm is not only about stress reduction. For example, sending JC to a meditation class isn't really going to support her with the health insurance company issues she is having, or help Devi and Elliot understand the treatment issues Dan is facing in France.

Some thought needs to go into what you can offer someone who is overwhelmed, what is appropriate at that point in time, what they are ready for, and what they can manage. Rather than thinking in terms of programs for overwhelmed people, I recommend crafting your own philosophy of care. You will need to create a philosophy of care specifically for working with the overwhelmed client. Your philosophy of care needs to be a little different for someone who is experiencing overwhelm than for clients who are not.

There are three essential elements in establishing your philosophy of care for a person who is overwhelmed. They are: how to listen; how to stop problem solving; and how to connect with resources. The next three sections will explore each of these elements so that you can create your own philosophy of care. I think of these three elements as getting a life jacket on someone who is overwhelmed.

Listen

In healthcare and human services, your ability to see and acknowledge the overwhelm may be the most helpful thing you can do. Overwhelm can be hard to recognize or acknowledge when you are in it. Sometimes people say the words, "I'm overwhelmed," but they are unable to identify or express the things that are making them feel overwhelmed.

It helps when providers acknowledge the overwhelm by saying, "You are overwhelmed. This is an incredibly difficult situation." As you witness and listen to a person's story, you are creating a place to put the overwhelm. A place that is outside of the person. You are helping them hold the overwhelm. When you listen, they are not alone.

It takes time to listen in this way. I think about listening to someone's story like sitting around a campfire. It is a quiet space, and someone is telling their story. When you "campfire" and listen to someone's story, you are creating a container for the overwhelm.

You may have no idea how to fix or help or resolve any of it, and you don't need to. Your first job is to listen.

In healthcare and human services we treat, we help, we try things, we figure things out. But I have learned with overwhelm that people need time to be heard, time to tell us about it. Even though you can't do anything to fix their problems, don't be afraid to ask your clients to tell you about them. Any person working in healthcare and human services can listen. Listening, receiving, and understanding are things you can do. When your client is too overwhelmed "to do" anything, listening is the most important thing you can offer.

As you listen, you will learn things about this person's overwhelm and their abilities. You will discover how strong they are, what they have tried, how they have suffered. You will see their compassion and their love for others. Overwhelmed people are often trying to care for someone else. You will learn how they ended up with problems that feel insurmountable.

You may discover that you don't know how they will recover from the overwhelm. You may not know how to solve any of it. But don't get distracted with solutions. Just pay attention to the quality of listening and attentiveness you are offering. You do not need to be a counselor or therapist to listen.

*At every stage of someone accessing healthcare
and human services, there is an opportunity
to listen, to campfire with someone.*

Listening is integral to serving clients in healthcare and human services. For me, listening begins with the first phone call. When I return a phone call to a prospective client, I am prepared to spend time on the phone with them. Think about your work. When does listening start for you?

Many of our systems in healthcare and human services may actually be set up to deflect listening. There are machines, messages, holding music, transfers. Think about how many calls or attempts an overwhelmed person must make before finding someone who listens to them.

I once received a call from a person who was assaulted in a domestic violence situation. I met with her and was able to convince her to go to the emergency room for her injuries. I let her know I would check in later that day to give her some emergency numbers she could call. Before giving her the phone numbers, I tested the numbers by calling myself. I wanted to be sure that it was actually possible for her to reach a person who could listen if she called. I wanted to know the numbers worked through the night and on weekends. The first hotline number I called did not connect me to a person. It was a message letting me know it operated only during certain hours. I tried a different hotline number that did connect to a support person at all hours and gave the client that number instead.

Very often people who are overwhelmed may have tried to connect to us but did not get anywhere. Our systems may be overwhelmed. Our programs may be full. Our help may not be available. Overwhelmed people may not keep trying.

Healthcare and human services providers are often under pressure to reduce time spent listening to clients. Our appointments are managed by minutes. A twenty-minute medical appointment, a fifty-minute hour therapy session—our listening time gets ever shorter. Sufficient time to listen and understand the overwhelm is an important support for an overwhelmed client. This is not the place to reduce or cut time. You may find that it is more helpful to have extra time with an overwhelmed client so they don't feel rushed or pressured.

Listening can be tiring. If your job involves a lot of listening, it is important to take breaks during the day and use other senses. Switch to reading, eating, or walking in short intervals during the day. When you go home at the end of a day of listening, you may find it difficult to have conversations with family members or to talk on the phone. You may need a listening break before sitting down to listen with your family. Do yoga together, cook, have family reading time, go outside together. Intentionally balancing the use of your senses helps you refuel.

Take time to reflect:

- When does listening start for you?

- How can you listen to someone who is overwhelmed, even if you are not a counselor?

- Think about a client you worked with who was overwhelmed. How much of their story did you hear?

Stop problem solving

In the previous chapter, we reviewed the first step when you are with an overwhelmed person: listen. But what do you do after you listen? Your job often necessitates that you do something. When someone is overwhelmed, we usually respond by trying to treat something or fix something, much like we would do if someone was having a heart attack or a real emergency.

You may look at your professional skills and wonder if these fit when faced with an overwhelmed client. Sometimes, the skills you offer may not really address the overwhelming situation you are hearing about. No matter what field of service you offer, the very next step after listening is to help the overwhelmed person stop problem solving.

That may sound crazy to you. An overwhelmed person is drowning in problems, and I am saying, "Let's help them stop problem solving." The irony is that when someone is overwhelmed, we tend to focus on problem solving. However, due to the nature of the overwhelm, the person is suffering from weak or broken problem-solving skills. What we need to do as a nurse, doctor, physical therapist, or psychotherapist is to address the brain and body that are under attack.

Being overwhelmed is like trying to play tennis with a broken arm or jog with a broken leg. If your arm was broken, we would put it in a cast and allow it time to be still and heal. The same thing is needed for a mind that is overwhelmed.

When someone is overwhelmed,
they need help to rest their brain.

Resting the mind is a very tricky concept. First of all, your mind is always going. It is not something you can put in a cast and hold still. But if we don't let the mind take a break from solving problems, it can't recover. The effects of stress on the brain will just make all problem solving less and less possible.

Research on the brain shows the part of the brain affected by stress is the ventral medial prefrontal cortex.[1] This is the part of the brain where decision making takes place. Your entire philosophy of care needs to address the fact that when a person is under too much stress, they can't problem solve. Notice how difficult it is when you have personal problems going on at home and you are helping people with problems all day at work. You

---

1 "Prior studies have shown consistently that repeated and chronic stress causes great damage to neural structures, connections, and functions of the prefrontal cortex, the seat of higher order cognition that helps regulate emotions, and more primitive areas of the brain." Yale Stress Center, Yale University (2016).

are vulnerable to mistakes, to burnout, and exhaustion when you are facing problems at work and at home.

Very few people understand what rest is or how to rest. You need to take the time to explain exactly what it means to stop problem solving and how to let the mind rest. Your explanation may be met with resistance.

"I can't rest, I can't even sleep at night."

"I don't have time to rest."

"Everything will fall apart if I rest."

When that occurs, help the overwhelmed person overcome their resistance and obstacles to resting in the context of their specific situation. I will honestly say it has taken weeks of repetition to help a client understand and integrate this concept.

Most people think if they just keep pushing onward, they will solve the problem and get past it. But that is not reality. The harder they push, the more stress they pile on and the more pressure they place on their mind and body. Ultimately, this will result in a longer recovery time, not a shorter one.

The goal is to stop the mind from problem solving. Let's return to the story about JC. JC's loss of her employment and healthcare coverage and the changes in her cancer treatment were overwhelming her. As her therapist, I discussed ways to take a short break from problem solving. Tackling problems from a mental state of overwhelm was not going to help her. The pressure to make choices and decisions while she was stressed was going to tax her brain further, and she would suffer more negative consequences. My goal was to help JC get her brain in a cast and to hold off on trying to solve her problems. During that time, she could practice resting and self-care.

Self-care is extremely hard to do when you are overwhelmed. It is important to ask your clients, "What do you do for self-care, nurturance, and enjoyment? At what point in the day or night can you do some self-care?"

Usually when I ask about self-care, overwhelmed people say, "What is that?" or, "I don't have time for that!"

When you hear that your client does not know what self-care is, notice your response. Do you feel inclined to make a joke? Do you silently blame them for their lack of self-care? Do you take it seriously that this is a critical skill for your client?

How effective are any of our strategies, interventions, or supports if a person is lacking self-care skills? When a person lacks self-care skills, you need to think in beginner steps. I call these easy on-ramps. All self-care skills can be thought of on a continuum. Self-care skills are learned; they are not automatic.

If you are working with an overwhelmed highly stressed person, you may think it makes sense to suggest they do some things for stress reduction. There is great research and incredibly effective strategies for stress reduction, such as mindfulness-based stress reduction, meditation, and journaling about feelings. However, there is a big glitch: all of these techniques take time to practice and take effect. People are often referred to try these things when they are at the peak of distress. Many will not follow up with yet another thing to do when they are overwhelmed. Others will try meditation, for example, and then report it didn't work. Stress reduction techniques won't work right away.

It is important to prepare people to understand that all stress reduction for the mind takes time to take effect.

Every person working in healthcare and human services needs to be trained in stress reduction and how it works. You will be explaining this to your clients many times, so you need to understand it and practice it yourself. Just as there are many opportunities to listen in healthcare and human services, there are many opportunities to take a few minutes to practice stress reduction with your clients.

Take a few minutes to do the stress reduction together.

Instead of problem solving, we are focusing our clients on resting the mind and learning stress reduction skills. These don't solve the problems, but they are meant to relieve the physical and mental stress on the overwhelmed person. It can be beneficial to do stress relieving activities when you are face-to-face with your clients. There are many easy stress busters you can do in just a few minutes with your clients. It does not take specialized training, and you are not going to hurt anyone by quietly taking a few minutes to breathe with someone or share some crayons and color.

Before we start, I typically say, "We just talked about some hard things. Let's take a few minutes and do a few minutes of stress reduction." Here are some of the stress relievers I do with clients:

- Three-minute meditations, where we sit with our eyes closed and breathe. Or I play a guided meditation from SoundsTrue.com that we follow. I also might read a meditation from Thich Nhat Hahn.

- Three-minute sound meditation using music for meditation

- Drawing an object that is in my office

- Coloring

- Vagus nerve stimulation. This nerve is in two-way communication with the brain. It touches every organ involved in an anxiety response. You can learn to make contact with this nerve by softening the hips and relaxing the sit bones and perineum in as short a time as two minutes.[2]

I highly recommend that you learn and practice proven methods of relaxation to help people physically relax. While I wish everyone would follow up with a one-hour massage, attend a yoga class, or take the time for a walk outside, telling people to do these things is not always going to feel possible for someone who is overwhelmed. But you can begin by sharing a baby step, something doable.

Getting someone started is something you can do. Yes, I will color with a client in my office. Showing someone how three minutes of relaxation feels can create a possibility for them. I know it is effective when clients say, "I can do this!" or "I'm stopping to buy crayons on my way home."

---

2 I learned this in a training led by Eric Gentry, Ph.D, International Association of Trauma Professionals.

The goal is to get someone to do fifteen minutes of self-care each day. Frances Marcus Lewis, a University of Washington Professor of Nursing Leadership, has shown that if you can get someone to do fifteen minutes of self-care daily, they will expand the amount of time thereafter. You just have to get them to start doing the first fifteen minutes.[3]

Take time to reflect:

- What stress busters can you teach in under five minutes with your patients and clients?

- What resources for brief relaxation techniques can you give to your clients to take with them?

---

3 Lewis, Frances Marcus. "Caring for the Caregivers," TEDxSnoIsleLibraries. Published January 12, 2016. https://www.youtube.com/watch?v=duhJHedj82g.

Be a spider

When someone is overwhelmed, they may need our support to find the help they need. An overwhelmed client may find it hard to call a referral and make appointments without some assistance. It is crucial that we listen to overwhelmed people to assess priorities. Determining where to begin gets really confusing when a client is overwhelmed.

Let's revisit Devi. She is suffering from a head injury and trying to get to her comatose boyfriend who is in another country. Helping her organize information and prioritize her next steps will be very important. Devi is also too overwhelmed to prioritize her own care. Reviewing with her what she needs for her own care and helping her prioritize her next steps for her care will also be useful.

I will help her connect to her doctor. She looks like she is in pain. She goes to the bathroom twice during our session. I will ask her to see her primary care person and text me so that I will know she is scheduled for an appointment. I will offer to contact her doctor and will provide some information to ensure that her doctor knows Devi is overwhelmed.

I am intervening in the overwhelm to show Devi I care about what is happening. I will take an extra step or two to let

Devi know she deserves some care. I will ask about other potential resources in her life, such as friends and family. I will see if there is someone else who can provide extra support.

I later discover that Devi has not been able to take care of herself. When I check in with her doctor, I learn that Devi has missed her last three appointments. As I talk on the phone about what Devi has been going through, her doctor goes from being frustrated with her lack of follow-through to deeply concerned and wanting to help her.

Whenever a person is overwhelmed, they can get so focused on trying to help save other people that they lose track of caring for themselves. When I step in to show some care and take an extra step or two to help, Devi will see that she matters, that I care about her. That care could motivate Devi to start caring just a bit more for herself.

You may be thinking, "I don't have time to do this for all my clients." I do not do this for all of my clients. I only do this with clients who meet the definition of overwhelmed. What I do with a client who is overwhelmed is completely different than what I do with a client who is not.

We don't want overwhelmed clients carrying the problem load by themselves.

So, you've acknowledged your client is overwhelmed, you have listened, you've helped them understand the need for mental rest, for a break from problem solving, and you have modeled some simple stress busters. But then what do you do with all the overwhelm? Most overwhelmed people need resources. The best treatment you can offer is vetted referrals to good resources to help with the overwhelm.

You will need a referral list for things you do not treat. You may not have a list or know who to refer to, and you may feel overwhelmed at the concept of creating one. It takes time working in the field to create a referral list. Give yourself time to gradually build this list.

Your referral list should include people with a variety of specializations. You may or may not know the people on your referral list. Your referral list can be developed from recommendations from people you know and trust. I always add people to my referral list based on my clients' recommendations.

My referral list includes doctors, nurse practitioners, physical therapists, psychiatrists, child and couples counselors, support groups, treatment programs, lawyers, financial planners, and bookkeepers. Financial planners and bookkeepers may seem outside of the human service or healthcare service network, but I have learned that money can be a big stressor and a source of overwhelm. I also keep a list of therapists I recommend in case my practice is full. I keep my lists within reach and on my phone. I know a nurse practitioner who has referral list handouts for her clients.

When someone calls me for counseling, I assume they are not feeling well. No one calls me because everything is going great. I feel a responsibility, even when I am full and can't see new patients, to provide a resource list of other counselors who can be called. An overwhelmed client may have trouble persisting in finding an available counselor. Some clinicians will have a message on their phone that clearly announces they are full and unable to accept new patients. This can add to a person's overwhelm. Please offer some direction on where to get a list of other counselors if you are full.

Callers often tell me that they don't have any other names or that people haven't called them back. I think it is a sign, a red flag, that counselors are too overwhelmed to respond when new clients call. Before you give a name of a resource to an overwhelmed client, it helps if you make a call and check to see if they are taking new referrals. Does their answering machine sound welcoming? I have called some places and heard the most unwelcoming phone messages.

Is your client a fit for what that practitioner does? Do you feel you are making a good match between the client and the resource? Based on brain research, we know that people who are overwhelmed have trouble making decisions. It helps if you do some screening of those on your referral list. For example, some of the nurse practitioners and doctors who refer to me know that if I am full, I will always provide some direction to find another counselor.

The benefit of your network is to get your overwhelmed client more wraparound care in a timely way.

In addition to your referral list, you should create a referral network. Your network is a group of providers who you know and who you may collaborate with to provide patient care. Working within a referral network means there will be prioritization to serve your clients. For example, if I am working with a person where there has been a recent death in a family and children are in the family, I will call someone in my network to ask if they can prioritize seeing the children. It means they will not be waiting for an appointment. It means their therapy will begin right away.

The network works both ways. Not only will my network prioritize treating someone in my care, I will prioritize someone in their care when they call. I prioritize within my network of treating providers so that the providers don't become overwhelmed if they can't get the full range of care managed for their client.

Establishing a network allows you to work more effectively with overwhelmed clients and prevent an avalanche of additional overwhelm.

You will be investing in building relationships with your referral network. It may take time to find the people you trust and believe work well with overwhelmed clients. You may need to try some unknowns and invest some time in getting to know people. Some providers are great with certain clients but lose patience with overwhelmed clients. You need to be sure you are sending clients to providers who have the capacity to work with an overwhelmed client. I had a client report back that a provider was yelling at her. I called the provider to check on the facts. The provider said, "I just got fed up. I was yelling." It takes some sorting to figure out who has the capacity to work with an overwhelmed client.

At different times, depending on my caseload, I have one to three primary care practices that I back up. This means when someone has a patient come in for care and is worried about the level of depression or anxiety, they will refer that person to me. Whatever the reason, the primary care person is concerned about the emotional well-being of the person. I prioritize these callers and save emergency slots in my weekly schedule for such calls.

You can't promise timely services with too many other colleagues or you will become overwhelmed.

When I work with overwhelmed people, I want to make appointments and referrals to other providers go as smoothly and easily as possible. I want people who know how to help, aren't overwhelmed themselves, and are responsive to calls. In return, I too am highly responsive to calls from someone in my referral network. If they are calling me, they are trying to urgently move someone in for help, and I need to respond quickly, get the information, and begin to triage.

I triage with my network.

My network of doctors, nurse practitioners, and physician assistants can reach me by text. I respond usually within an hour. If I can't get the person in to see me, I will help them get to see someone with expertise in my network. We are all trying to make the calls easier on the client because the client may be too overwhelmed.

I was working with a mom whose daughter had died. She mentioned that she wasn't feeling well and had blood in her stool. Unfortunately, her doctor had left her practice, so mom didn't have a doctor. I gave her the name of a physician and asked if she would call the doctor. She told me she didn't want to see a new physician because they would ask questions, and she didn't want to tell them about her daughter. She told me she couldn't stop crying, and she couldn't handle how people looked at her.

I suggested that I call the doctor for her. I said I would tell them about the loss of her daughter and ask that they not mention it. I would advise them to focus only on the blood in her stool. She agreed to this plan. When I called a physician in my network to relay information about this mom, I heard back the same day.

When I call resources in my network, I typically hear back no later than the next morning. Because of our professional relationship, if I give my name to a receptionist, I am usually patched right through to my colleague. Inside this referral network, we often use personal cell phones to make connecting easier, so I rarely need to go through a reception desk. This goes both ways; they have my cell phone number, too.

Your network becomes a safety net for some of the most overwhelmed and vulnerable people. As you build a network, you are going to get more referrals, and they may be sending you overwhelmed clients. You need to think about how many referral connections you can support in this way. You will experience some pressure from your network to respond. You need to be honest about what you can handle. You need to structure your schedule to know how many of these referrals you can accommodate.

You need to know when someone needs a different care provider or a higher level of care than you can provide.

In my referral network, I have two psychiatrists, two psychiatric nurses, and two people with Ph.Ds. This is the part of my network I refer to as the higher level of care. When I am working with a client who is beyond my level of expertise, I will refer them to someone in my network who has more expertise. In some cases, I collaborate with them; we create a joint treatment plan and decide who does what. If necessary, I will transfer them because I do not know how to treat the issues the person is having.

Only you know what you are able to treat and when you need to send a client to someone with a higher level of care or more experience. You can learn a lot by finding out how the higher level of care provider treated the client. You may want to consider enrolling in training courses to learn new skills. There is a fine line between learning something new and working way outside of your sandbox of what you know.

You will notice that you feel overwhelmed by a client if you are working with someone who is beyond your abilities.

You will get symptoms of your own overwhelm from working with someone beyond your level of care. You will feel stress and distress. Pay attention to those feelings. It is an indication that you need a consultation, possibly supervision, and perhaps a referral for your client.

It is not a sign of failure to know your limits. The criteria I use for a referring is:

- Beyond what I know how to treat
- Unable to treat client in an outpatient office setting in hourly sessions; client may need inpatient care

---

Be prepared that connections to certain resources may fail or be short-lived.

You will need to have realistic expectations about resources and other providers. It can be frustrating and disappointing when the resource doesn't work. Don't give up on building resources when the client gives up or the services go away. Move on to new possibilities when something doesn't work. These resources become life changing when they do work out. It will take persistence and a don't-give-up attitude.

Many resources—nonprofit organizations and support groups—do not have stable funding. Your resource may have high staff turnover. I acknowledge the disappointment when a connection doesn't work out with a client. However, the difference between me and the client at that moment is that I have more persistence than they do. I will loan them some of mine to try again. I will help them not give up. It is not helpful if I give up on finding resources too. Finding additional supports is extremely difficult. But the journey is worth it. When a resource works well for someone, it will help immensely.

Put into practice:

- **Create your referral list.** Be sure to have a phone number for each person on your list. At the end of your page, list the type of referrals you should add to your list in the near future. Add new referral names and numbers when you hear recommendations about them from clients and colleagues. In your professional organizations, ask others who they refer to. Think about the people you personally use for massage, physical therapy, acupuncture as possible referrals. Challenge yourself to keep growing your list.

- **Create your referral network.** Begin by establishing a connection to someone who is referred to you by another professional. Get a release and call that referral. Ask if there is anything they want you to know. Send them a progress report in a month. This begins a process of building a connection to another professional.

- If you already have a referral network, assess your list of names and see if you are being responsive enough to this network. Have you given them easy access to you? Do you have backdoor access to these people?

- Use resources if you work in an agency. Ask other people in your organization who they refer to and see if they will share their list.

- Reach out. Whether building a referral network or a referral list, take a potential colleague to lunch or coffee. Make time to talk and get to know your colleagues and community providers.

Discussing boundaries

As I became more experienced dealing with overwhelming situations, I learned that boundaries were fundamental to helping the clients who were overwhelmed. I found myself modeling boundaries, talking about boundaries, writing and teaching about boundaries. I created a way of teaching this life skill and wrote a book that anyone can use to learn how to use their boundaries. I have heard feedback from all around the globe that this way of teaching boundaries works.

When a client is under tremendous stress, they will feel like or believe they don't have any boundaries. Here are some boundary truths you can tell your clients:

- We always have boundaries
- You can't ever lose them
- Boundaries come from inside of you
- They are made of your yeses and noes
- Listen to your boundaries and say no where you need to

When you help an overwhelmed client reconnect to their yes and no, you are helping to treat the overwhelm. Give your clients permission to say no where they need to. Do not tell your client where to set a boundary. Do not tell them where they should say no. This is not how boundary building works.

Do not tell an overwhelmed client your personal story of being overwhelmed and how you got through it. I believe there is a time and place to connect with your clients and be real, but not when you are working with an overwhelmed client. When your client is overwhelmed with their own story, it is important not to burden them by sharing your heavy story. It is harmful to the overwhelmed client to add more emotional pain when they are already hurting. Remember you are there to listen to your client.

Boundaries are key to recovery for overwhelm. I begin boundary skill building with self-care skills. Next, I work on understanding boundaries and feelings. Last, we work on setting boundaries where needed. There are many steps to being able to effectively use boundaries. When you point your clients towards the resources to learn boundary skills, you are helping them recover from some of the overwhelm and learning how to prevent some of the overwhelm in the future. Notice I said "some." Not all overwhelm can be prevented. But boundary skills are fundamental to recovery and prevention.

If you are not an expert at teaching boundary skills, please refer your client to resources that can help them learn to build their boundaries. I have a book, an app, a TEDx talk online, and online classes, as do others in this field. Find some resources you like on boundaries and recommend a resource to help your clients think about their boundaries.

Put into practice:

- Read at least two self-help book on boundaries.

- My book, *Transform Your Boundaries*, and my website, SarriGilman.com, have resources online that you can share.

- Find some resources on boundary building that you can share with your clients.

Notes:

_____

_____

_____

_____

_____

_____

_____

_____

_____

_____

_____

_____

_____

_____

PART II:

Getting a Life Jacket on You, the Provider

Notes:

_____

_____

_____

_____

_____

_____

_____

_____

_____

_____

_____

_____

_____

_____

_____

CHAPTER THREE:

What is Care Provider Overwhelm

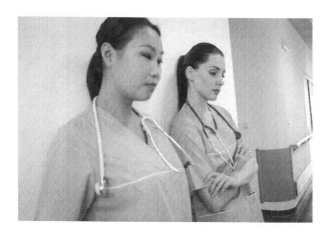

"I order the cultures, prescribe an antidiarrheal drug and some dietary modifications, briefly mention psychotherapy again, and leave the room. Then I sit at my workstation to document and bill for our encounter, perched at the edge of my seat, on the verge of despair."–Dr. Suzanne Koven[4]

---

4 Suzanne Koven, "The Doctor's New Dilemma," New England The Journal of Medicine, N Engl J Med 2016; 374: 608-609; February 18, 2016; DOI: 10.1056; NEJMp1513708.

Story about Mira

Mira works for a nonprofit organization. She was hired to work with clients and initially told her caseload would be twenty to twenty-five people in a month. Reality has been very different. Mira finds herself struggling to attend to sixty-five to seventy-five clients monthly. She was offered a raise of fifty cents an hour to take on managerial tasks as well. She is supervising new staff, attending community meetings, and seeing her clients. The organization where she works has lost their human resources person, and Mira is asked to cover those duties for four months along with another staff member.

It takes Mira a lot of time to figure out which part of the human resources job she is doing and which part the other staff is covering. Sometimes there is confusion, and Mira feels she is doing her job inadequately. She isn't trained in human resources or supervision, and she finds herself guessing how to handle things.

Mira is having trouble sleeping. She finds herself worrying all night about her clients and about how to handle situations at work. She gets to work early and leaves late. She isn't even sure what her work hours are or when her day begins or ends. It just feels endless. She finds herself returning client calls late into the evening.

Mira feels like things are slipping through the cracks and that she isn't doing anything well or right. She is so depleted by her job that she has no social life outside of work. She is struggling to pay her bills. Everyone she works with seems stressed and overworked.

Think about this situation:

- When have you felt your caseload was too large?

- How does it impact you when you have too many clients?

- What situations do you see your clients experiencing that are very close to home for you or your family?

- When have you felt stressed at your job? What were the circumstances?

Overwhelm spreads

People working in healthcare and human services are vulnerable to overwhelm. Mira's story is not unusual. Many people working in healthcare and human services are feel overwhelmed. Despite the literature and research on compassion fatigue, secondary trauma, and self-care, there is a disconnect between "what we know" and "what we do" to prevent overwhelm in healthcare and human services.

There are a couple of reasons for this. In an article published by the American Counseling Association (ACA),[5] wellness experts, founders of The Resiliency Center, and therapists who have served on committees focused on these issues for counselors. The information they shared can easily apply to anyone working in the helping professions. According to the article, "Although most counselors are familiar with self-care—even preaching the concept religiously to a client—many find it a challenge to put the concept into practice in their own lives. Wellness experts say as life gets busy, counselors may tend

---

5 Lynne Shallcross, "Taking Care of Yourself as a Counselor," Counseling Today, American Counseling Association, http://ct.counseling.org/2011/01/taking-care-of-yourself-as-a-counselor.

to assume that they can, or even should, handle problems and stress on their own."[6]

According to Gerard Lawson, previous chair of the ACA Task Force on Counselor Wellness and Impairment, "People who end up in helping professions are naturally inclined to take care of others."[7] Sandra Rankin, an ACA member with her own private practice, states, "The work itself can stand in the way of wellness. Many counselors struggle just to get through the day, so self-care takes a backseat to limited time and fatigue. Plus, some work environments make it difficult for therapists to engage in self-care because of unusual or long work hours, large caseloads and little or no support."[8]

Healthcare and human services are faced with meeting overwhelming needs and overwhelmed people all the time. Contact with overwhelmed people does have an effect on you. Working in this field, you are around not only overwhelmed clients, but overwhelmed coworkers as well. There may be a relentless intensity surrounding you. If you have anything going on in your personal life, such as a divorce, a sick family member, or a death in your family, the stress on you is even greater.

---

6 Id.
7 Id.
8 Id.

We have a word in healthcare and human services, a word we are supposed to be aspiring towards, a word that insists we can protect ourselves. That word is "resiliency." Those of us who work in the field are supposed to be "resilient." But what does resilient mean?

The American Psychological Association (APA) defines resilience as "the process of adapting well in the face of adversity, trauma, tragedy, threats or even significant sources of stress." While this definition is useful, it does not reflect the complex nature of resilience.[9] Determinants of resilience include a host of biological, psychological, social, and cultural factors that interact with one another to determine how one responds to stressful experiences.

I prefer Catherine Panter-Brick's definition of resilience: "Resilience is the process to harnessing biological, psychosocial, structural and cultural resources to sustain wellbeing."[10] I prefer her definition because she describes resilience as a process, which describes the ongoing nature of cultivating resilience.

---

9 For a discussion on resiliency, see "Resilience," S.M. Southwick, H. Douglas-Palumberi, and R.H. Pietrzak, in J.J. Friedman, T.M. Keane, and P.A. Resick, eds., Handbook of PTSD: Science and Practice, 2d ed. (New York: Guilford Press, 2014).
10 Catherine Panter-Brick, James F. Leckman, "Editorial Commentary: Resilience in Child Development—Interconnected Pathways to Wellbeing, J Child Psychology and Psychiatry, Vol. 54, Issue 4 (April 2013): 333-336, http://onlinelibrary.wiley.com/doi/10111/jcpp.12057/full.

It also implies an understanding that it is a process, not a static way of being. People who work in healthcare and human services see adversity every single day and nearly every hour. If you think deeply about what that means, the description as a process of harnessing resources actually feels incredibly supportive and helpful to our field.

We use the word "resilient" like it is a shield, or cure, and certainly as an expectation for anyone who works in health and human services.

The expectation that healthcare and human service workers are supposed to be more resilient than other human beings is absurd. The idea that every person working in our field comes to work resilient is a myth. Our passion and insistence on the idea of resiliency may also create shame around anyone in our field experiencing overwhelm. If you get overwhelmed and it is too much— you are stressed, your problem solving is decreasing, you are struggling, you find yourself quietly tolerating your distress—you fear someone will see your distress and you won't appear "resilient." As you pretend to be resilient, your overwhelm may be increasing.

How do we recognize when ourselves, our healthcare team, our human service providers are overwhelmed? It is possible that you can be a resilient person and you may also have times when you are feeling overwhelmed.

Resilient people may be a bit more vulnerable to overwhelm because you may be expecting yourself to cope and handle hard things.

You may not recognize when you are becoming overwhelmed. You may not notice that you are short-tempered, unable to shift or downsize your load, never feeling like you can take a break. Because you are distracted, depleted, or unable to focus or be responsive to others, you may not be able to help your clients. Though the truth has been out for a long time that people in health and human services are vulnerable to burnout and vicarious trauma, there is still the expectation or assumption that it won't happen to you.

I have worked in our field for thirty years. I work very hard every day to protect myself from overwhelm. It doesn't take too much to find myself overscheduled. The tipping point is very small; one or two extra clients in a day and I will be working overtime. I will also begin a vicious cycle of overscheduling that will take a long time to recover from because having too many clients on my caseload means a few extra hours each day for months. To protect myself from this, I strive to be vigilant about my schedule every single day. Even with thirty years of experience, before I schedule a new client, I ask myself, "Am I leaving time for me to refuel, eat, rest, and play at the end of the day? Does the day have a stop point?"

There is a huge expectation that anyone who works in health and human services knows how to protect themselves from being overwhelmed. This is not true. The work you do every day puts some stress on you. You may feel you could use some stress reduction yourself. Look for ways in which you can improve your own stress reduction. Certain tasks, certain clients, your commute, or certain times of the day may be more stressful than others. Stress management is a continuous process. It is always good to ask yourself if you need some stress reduction and what you can do to make your life and your work less stressful.

You may not even be responsible for overloading yourself. A coworker may leave a job, and you may be asked to cover their clients temporarily. People in our field are expected to do fifty-plus hour workweeks. Nurses on sixteen-hour shifts, people being asked to cover an extra caseload when someone else is on medical leave, and high staff turnover results in extra work and an extra load on you.

I have a deep concern that burnout is a negative label that implies that somehow you did something wrong as a provider. The word doesn't accurately reflect that the system may be burning you out. We need to change the expectations we have about the resiliency of providers. Of course, there will be times when you are overwhelmed. There are many factors creating overwhelm all around you in healthcare and human services.

It is normal for there to be times when you feel overwhelmed.

How can you recognize when you are overwhelmed? How can you take steps to help yourself without feeling shame? How can you fully realize that in order to stay in the healthcare field, you must care for yourself and protect yourself vigilantly against the tide of overwhelm that surrounds you every day? In the following sections, we will review specific ways to care for yourself and protect yourself from getting overwhelmed.

Take time to reflect:

- Write a list of all the things you do at your job. Include of all of your responsibilities.

- Add to the list all of your responsibilities at home.

- Place a star next to each responsibility that at times can become overwhelming.

Caring for your feelings

When I was training to become a therapist, the grad school I attended required each student to be in therapy. It was my first time in therapy. Therapy is where I learned to decipher my feelings. In the family where I grew up, not a single family member was able to discuss their emotions. We were certainly having emotional experiences, but in my family these emotions were acted out in a terrifying way. Feelings were never discussed, explored, or understood. I had to learn these skills in grad school therapy training and in personal therapy. I also continue three decades later to add to my toolset. As research comes out, I continue to learn and practice ways to understand feelings.

Many of you may not have had the opportunity to learn about emotions, deeply explore your own feelings in therapy, or develop a toolset for all the feelings you experience while doing your job. Every person working in healthcare and human services needs a regular set of daily practices to care for their feelings. As a care provider, you are guiding and supporting people. You have decisions to make as you guide people. If you are overwhelmed, your judgment and decisions will be affected.

*Caring for your feelings is a way to
enhance and develop your resiliency.*

You may not be aware of this shift. Some people don't realize their judgment or decisions are off. Your coworkers probably will notice. Your clients will be impacted. You may notice and not know why you are struggling. You may not recognize that you are overwhelmed.

Your emotions also will be impacted from being overwhelmed. You may experience an emotional storm of feelings that can feel like too much to navigate at once or for one person to navigate alone. While you are experiencing your own emotional storm, you are working with overwhelmed people who are agitated with their own tangle of emotions that may include fear, frustration, grief, exhaustion, anger, resentment, impatience, sorrow, regret, trauma, and depression.

*You may find yourself wanting to
avoid the large swell of emotions.*

You need strategies to care for your emotions. You need strategies to interact with clients who are overwhelmed. Avoiding unsettling feelings may seem like the only way to cope.

There are lots of ways people avoid feeling. You may find yourself numbing out in front of a screen, drinking, taking pills, avoiding contact with friends or family, or isolating yourself. Over time, numbing out, trying not to feel, and isolating will actually make you sick. Your feelings don't leave you. Whatever you avoid or ignore stays inside of you and waits. Your feelings will wait for you to face them.

Many people become depressed or anxious as their unexamined feelings pile up inside. The best thing you can do to protect and help yourself is to have a strategy to know and understand your feelings.

Notes:

_____

_____

_____

_____

_____

_____

_____

CHAPTER FOUR:

Protecting Yourself from Overwhelm

Dealing with the gray cloud

There are times when your emotions will accumulate like a thick gray storm cloud. You may feel "charged" with emotion. When you are emotionally charged, you may not feel as in control of your emotions. Your emotions seem to take over and you react strongly to those around you. You may be angry, hostile, impatient, and frustrated, and dump on people around with you with criticism and anger. When you are "charged," it is helpful to have coping strategies in place.

Strategies for understanding your feelings

One of the best ways to know your emotions is to write in a daily journal. There is excellent research that writing about your emotions is an essential way to stay connected to yourself and understand how you are feeling. According to a University of Auckland in New Zealand study, HIV/AIDS patients who journaled about their negative life experiences showed improved immune functioning that suggested journaling helped reduce their HIV-related anxiety.[11] One of the psychologists at the forefront of this research and a researcher in the New Zealand study, James Pennebaker, PhD, of the University of Texas at Austin, stated that, "By writing, you put some structure and organization to those anxious feelings. It helps you to get past them."[12] Pennebaker likens the benefits from journaling to those found in therapy. "People who talk about things over and over in the same ways aren't getting any better. There has to be growth or change in the way they view their experiences."[13]

---

11 See Bridget Murray, "Writing to Heal," American Psychological Association, Vol. 33, No. 6 (June 2002): 54, http://www.apa.org/monitor/jun02/writing.aspx.
12 Id.
13 Id.

When people change their perspective you can see it in the language they use, says Pennebaker. People appear to benefit more when they use words that are cause-and-effect words: "because," "realize," and "understand."[14] Some personality types respond better to writing than others.[15]

Here are some journaling tips:

- This is a safe place where you can vent. Your journal is not for publication; it is not something anyone else ever needs to read. It is for you. It is a safe place for you to recognize your feelings and write about them.

- Emotions can overwhelm your ability to think. When you get to know your emotions by writing, you can become a support person to yourself.

- It is easy to get too busy and ignore the need for journaling. Don't use it only if you are feeling terrible. Make journaling a daily practice.

- Capture all the warmth and uplifting feelings you have about your work and your life as well as the difficult things.

---

14 Id.
15 Id.

In addition to journaling, there are many well-researched benefits from meditating.[16] For people who work in healthcare and human services, it can help you reduce your mental stress and help you soothe your distressed emotions.

As you practice meditating, it will help you slow down and notice more of what you are experiencing. You can use meditation to gradually become more aware of your thoughts and feelings. This awareness can stop your emotions from building up into a storm. In your busy day and contact with clients, you are focused on other people. Meditation is a way to bring yourself home to you.

Some people find it soothing to have expressive outlets, like art, when they feel charged. Art, such as collage or painting, can be way to discharge and know your feelings. Take time with your art to notice how it connects to a specific experience you

---

16 See Sara W. Lazar, Ph.D, Lazar Lab for Meditation Research, Harvard University. Lazar and her colleagues have found that, "Mindfulness practice leads to increases in regional brain gray matter density. 1. The primary difference, we found in the posterior cingulate, which is involved in mind wandering, and self relevance; 2. The left hippocampus, which assists in learning, cognition, memory and emotional regulation; 3. The temporo parietal junction, or TPJ, which is associated with perspective taking, empathy and compassion; 4. An area of the brain stem called the Pons, where a lot of regulatory neurotransmitters are produced. The amygdala, the fight or flight part of the brain which is important for anxiety, fear and stress in general. That area got smaller in the group that went through the mindfulness-based stress reduction program. The change in the amygdala was also correlated to a reduction in stress levels."

had and your feelings about it. Other people exercise when they are charged. But it is not complete to just exercise and take the steam off, because the charge will return in a few hours.

With any of these strategies, however, you still need to sit with yourself and figure out **why** you are feeling charged. Are you feeling powerless? Exhausted? Frustrated that you have no time for yourself? What is it that has charged your emotions? Did someone insult you, hurt you, ignore something important? Did you witness something difficult? Was there a mistake? As you understand why you were emotionally charged, you can then figure out what options you have for dealing with the situation. But first take care of yourself and the emotional charge. It is not helpful to deal with a situation when you feel emotionally charged. Wait until you have taken time to understand your feelings and can feel the charge reduce.

You may need help understanding your feelings and reducing the charge you are feeling. Psychotherapy is another option for dealing with your emotions. It is important to have a safe place to talk about your feelings and be understood and supported. Talking to a counselor can help you with the emotions you are carrying from your work. Therapy is especially important to build resiliency. As you learn about yourself and experiences that have been difficult in your life, you can learn ways to care for yourself emotionally and explore the boundaries you may need to protect yourself from some of the overwhelm.

What if it doesn't help

When you first start doing these practices:—writing, meditation, psychotherapy—it may at first feel like they don't really help. People try meditating twice and report it didn't really do anything. Meditating isn't effective if you only do it twice. The same can be said for journaling, psychotherapy, or jogging. These practices are truly effective when you practice them. All of these practices take effect over time. You build up to their effectiveness by practicing. It is like brushing your teeth. You do it several times a day, not only when you have a cavity. And you still may get cavities, but you keep brushing your teeth.

This is the same with caring for your feelings. Creating a daily set of practices to care for your feelings does not mean you will never get overwhelmed. But your practices can help you recover from being overwhelmed. You can intervene and save yourself, know that you may need to increase your time taking care of yourself or add some additional things to help you, such as therapy as needed.

Your feelings want you to understand them. You don't have to act on every feeling. In fact, you may discover that your emotions are not necessarily the best way to express yourself, but it is a crucial way to understanding yourself and all that you are experiencing. Buried, ignored, unacknowledged feelings will create symptoms for you. Learning how to know your feelings, stay emotionally connected, and supportive of yourself will also allow you to be effective with your clients. You will be able to advise your clients to use strategies you know for sure are effective because you practice them too.

Put into practice:

- Write yourself a plan to improve your care for your feelings.

- What can you add in, start doing regularly?

- What are you willing to do to learn more about your emotions?

Notes:

_____

_____

_____

_____

_____

_____

CHAPTER FIVE:

The Need for Supervision and Mentoring

Supervision is a sacred relationship. I consider it a lifelong investment in someone. I learned about the idea of supervision being a sacred relationship from my supervisors. I was fortunate to start my career with supervisors who made this sort of investment and relationship with me.

I experienced supervision even before starting my career. I received supervision as part of my education to become a teacher and then a therapist. Supervision was "given" to me, and I believe it shaped me to be present with people and with myself in ways that would not have been possible otherwise. Supervision gave me:

- Skills in places where I had gaps

- Strength when I thought I should quit

- Compassion for others and the ability to look deeply at others

- Compassionate care for myself

- Capacity to do the work

Supervision is the legacy I will leave in our field, it is what I will pass along to others. It is what you will pass on to others, and it will be your legacy.

Supervision is an essential "listening" post for people who work in healthcare and human services.

Supervision for supervisees

Earlier in this book, I explained that listening is a crucial support for your clients who are overwhelmed. Listening is also a crucial support when you are overwhelmed. Working in healthcare and human services, you are expected to bring compassion to your work. In order to stay in healthy connection to your compassion, you need to be able to process the emotions that you are experiencing from your job. No person can express compassion all the time. You will experience other emotions too. You need a supervisor to share some of what you are witnessing. You need to have a supervisor who cares about you and the load you are carrying.

---

*It is not your job to carry the emotional weight
of your work on your shoulders in silence.*

It is part of your job to receive supervision during your working hours. Being supervised and discussing what you are witnessing and feeling is how to grow your resiliency. It may be hard to recognize the importance of supervision time when there are so many pressing needs competing for your attention. You may find it hard to protect your supervision time. You may think your time is better spent seeing a client with an urgent need or completing your charting. You may even think your supervisor wants you to see one more client or use the time instead to catch up on charting. Supervision time may become a diminished priority; however, supervision time is a significant way to prevent burnout, and the time must be prioritized and protected. If it seems as though all other things are more important than supervision and there is no time for you to have supervision, then that is a critical topic to discuss in supervision. Both you and your supervisor will need to commit to protect your supervision time.

Supervising you is how we prevent burning you out.
Supervising you is how you are mentored,
nurtured, and seen.

Supervision is not just for beginners. The essence of what you need from supervision will change over time. So, it is important for you to determine if your needs are being met in supervision. Only you will know if your supervisor is the right supervisor for you. It helps to ask yourself some questions and evaluate if your supervisor is helping you:

- Are you learning about your resiliency?

- Are you able to work with more complex and challenging situations?

- Do you feel like a weight has been lifted off your shoulders?

- Does your supervisor listen to you?

Given the precious time allotted to it, supervision needs to be well defined. If supervision time is crowded with too many expectations, the listening time can be sacrificed instead to manage paperwork and share organizational information. In task-focused supervision, you will find yourself listening to your supervisor, rather than being listened to and getting to share some of the load you are carrying. Task-focused supervision runs the risk of leaving you with more weight, rather than less, on your shoulders.

Group supervision may crowd the supervision time further, allowing even less time to be heard. While group supervision may develop clinical skills, it may not allow sufficient time for each person to debrief their overwhelming experiences. Without adequate time to process, supervision can actually add to the overwhelm you are experiencing.

Supervision needs to help you deal with the emotions you are having about the things you are witnessing as you care for others. Supervision is a place to talk about feelings. You may wonder if it is appropriate to talk about your feelings at work.

You are listening to feelings all the time in your job. It makes sense that you would discuss them in supervision. You need to have a designated time and space where it is okay to talk about your feelings.

Before you accept a job in a specific healthcare or human service organization, I recommend that you ask about the type of supervision they offer and who will be supervising you. It is also okay to ask in an interview how the organization prevents staff from getting overwhelmed, and what the organization does to help staff debrief following difficult experiences.

You may find that there are big differences between organizations in terms of what is offered for supervision and support.

Your supervision is an important line of defense to prevent you from getting overwhelmed, depleted, and exhausted.

The big elephant in the healthcare and human services room is that your supervisor may be depleted and overwhelmed, or too busy to provide supervision and support to you. If your supervisor is overwhelmed, you will find yourself trying to help or support your supervisor. You may also wish to avoid your overwhelmed supervisor. If your supervisor is overwhelmed, it doesn't mean you can go without supervision. In the previous chapter, I reviewed some of things you can and must provide for yourself, but supervision is something that needs to be provided to you.

If your organization cannot provide supervision, or can't provide someone who is not overwhelmed, you will suffer. This is a place where you will need boundaries to protect yourself. I am very aware that supervision is profoundly underresourced and may not be available within your organization. If you are not getting adequate support and supervision, it is okay to first discuss this with your supervisor. Is your supervisor able to hear your feedback and offer what you need? If not, can you be transferred to a different supervisor in the organization? If none is available, it is reasonable to quit the job and move to an organization that can provide you with supervision.

Supervision is not something you can go without and remain personally healthy in our field. Burnout is prevented and resiliency is developed not only by the steps you take, but by the type of supervision you receive. Show me a burned out staff person, and it tells me a lot about the kind of supervision they didn't get. You need support and supervision to remain healthy and do this work.

Activity *for supervisee:*

- Evaluate the quality of supervision you are getting.

- Do you have regular supervision at a scheduled, predictable time?

- Is there adequate time for your supervisor to listen and hear about the load you are carrying?

- Does your supervisor ask about your feelings?

- Is your supervisor overwhelmed?

- Is your supervisor a good listening post for you?

- What would improve supervision?

Supervision for supervisors

I am concerned that supervision is one of the areas in healthcare and human services that is burdened with too many responsibilities, and supervisors are unable to address the tasks and personal support needed. Supervision is not adequately resourced in many places. As a supervisor, the scope of your job is much more than supervising staff, and your job probably exceeds the hours you have to do your job.

You may find yourself with staff that are needing development and training to match the needs of the overwhelmed clients they are caring for. The clients may need more experienced staff than you have, or can afford to have, on your team. If the clients' needs are very high, even your experienced staff will need more support to manage the complexity of many high-need situations. Matching needs with staff abilities may not be possible in your circumstances. If there is a gap, you will find yourself helping your staff navigate through many situations, and doing lots of clinical case management and oversight for safety reasons.

There are many demands put on supervisors by upper management, supervisees, and regulators in the field, with the ultimate priority of assuring that client needs are being met.

Supervisors are dancing with many partners at once. As a supervisor, you may wonder if anyone is getting what they need from you.

It is beneficial for supervisors to collect staff feedback at regular intervals throughout the year to determine whether staff finds supervision time helpful in managing overwhelm and provides them with opportunities to discuss their feelings. Here are three questions you can use to collect feedback from supervisees:

- Do you feel you have enough supervision support from me?
- Are you getting to discuss your feelings and challenges in supervision?
- What else would be helpful to you?

When supervisors collect feedback, it serves as a way to ensure that supervision time is not filled with too much other business. If there is insufficient time in supervision or supervision is consumed with task management, it can actually be doing more harm than good.

Supervisors need to have the skill and commitment to talk about feelings with their team. Many supervisors earn their supervisory position inside their organizations based on their amount of time in the field or time with the agency. Supervisors may find themselves unprepared or unable to emotionally support their staff. All supervisors need training and practice to prevent staff overwhelm and debrief trauma, and to help frontline staff process emotions.

If a supervisor doesn't know how to provide a space for staff to emotionally process their experiences at work, staff may be getting the message that their feelings are not acceptable at work. Even worse, they may be told their feelings are inappropriate or that they are somehow wrong for having emotional responses while working in the healthcare or human services field.

If a supervisor is struggling with how to discuss feelings and provide staff support, training and coaching is needed to develop the supervisor's abilities to supervise. This investment to develop a supervisor may take time, but it is well worth it. Frontline staff who receive great supervision, will stay with the job and will eventually become supervisors who can provide quality supervision to the next generation.

If we go without adequate supervision in healthcare and human services, we could be damaging our capacity to provide it over decades because the line staff who don't receive it will not know how to provide it. There is an opportunity for foundations to help fund this under-resourced part of social and health services. Grants and private funding could address this hidden pervasive problem.

Supervisors also need support for themselves. It helps to have a mentor when you are a supervisor, especially when you are starting out in leadership. A mentor is an experienced supervisor who is available to listen to you, share ideas with, and will help you develop your supervisory and leadership skills.

Every supervisor needs a few colleagues who are also supervisors to debrief with and get support from. It can be isolating to be supervisor if you don't have a small circle of others who can support and discuss their work. Your support can be from colleagues who work in different organizations or within your own. It is important to have regular check-ins where the boundary of safety and privacy is maintained, where there is time to connect, and where colleagues have the capacity to share helpful ideas. Some of my colleagues over the years have become my closest support system.

Supervisors also need a personal reflecting process. So much is coming at you each day that you need some quiet time alone each day to reflect and think about the priorities of the day, think about interactions, think about where you may need to have a conversation. I carry a small journal with me to catch up with myself. This journal is neither a to-do list nor is it for meeting notes. It is just for notes with myself, a way to notice my own feelings and be with me.

All supervisors are vulnerable to overwhelm.

You never reach a point in healthcare and human services where you are "invincible" to overwhelm. The overwhelm disrupts your thinking capacity. If supervisors are overwhelmed, help and support from colleagues, as well as a complete break from the work, is needed. Taking a complete break from work may sound extreme and be scary, but it helps reinforce the boundaries, stops the constant input, and allows you to heal. It may be necessary to prevent additional physical and mental strain.

It is important that supervisors get counseling during the break. Allowing your mind to rest and be free of responsibilities helps you recover from overwhelm; counseling helps you understand your feelings and build your self-care plan. Then when you reengage with work, you can reprioritize, set boundaries around what you can and can't do, and take better care of yourself through each day.

Our field is human services, not superhuman services.

You don't have a cape or magic abilities. Unrealistic expectations need to be called out as such. It is not your job to endure unrealistic expectations. Supervisors are positioned to model realistic boundaries and well-being in organizations.

Activity for supervisors:

- What will you change about your supervision after reading this chapter?

- What can you do to increase the support for you as a supervisor?

- What boundaries do you need to address?

Notes:

_____

_____

_____

_____

_____

CHAPTER SIX:

Protecting Your Boundaries

There are three specific areas you must define and always pay attention to when you work in healthcare and human services: your time, your job description, and your role with clients. These areas require your constant attention because there is always a push for you to do more. If you are feeling overwhelmed, it is harder to manage these boundaries, and you will feel like you are being consumed alive. As we saw with Mira, the overwhelmed caseworker, her job grew and grew without any reduction in responsibilities.

Defining your time

I remember the day I realized that I was invited to so many meetings that it was impossible to attend them all. In my role at the agency, it felt impossible to decline the meetings. It also felt impossible to get my job done if I was attending meetings all the time. In addition, the meetings started early in the morning, with aggressive start times of 7:00 a.m. and late meetings started at 6:30 p.m. My days were being stretched longer and longer. As my days were stretched, the workweek stretched into weekends, and it seemed as though I was always working.

I learned in the human services field,
boundaries need to come from within.

When I peered in and looked at my feelings, I felt frustrated, obligated, and resentful that I had to attend the meetings. As the meeting demands continued to mount, they began to conflict and overlap with each other. Finally, I established my own criteria for attending a meeting, and I started responding to requests with, "I can't attend. I get invited to so many meetings that I absolutely never see my family. For me, my family time is precious." Then I established my own start and end time for each day. As I set my boundaries around meetings, I grew more confident in my ability to set boundaries in human services. Over time, colleagues, whom I initially feared saying "no" to, started reaching out and inviting me for coffee to ask me more about how to set limits and how to uphold their own boundaries.

Time is a precious resource.
Our field has boundary challenges with time.

In healthcare and human services, time management tools can seem useless because the problems are far more serious than time management. It has been accepted in this field that there will always be just too much to do, and you may not even notice overload because it is so common in our field. Learning to recognize overwhelm and talk about it may lead to managing it.

One of the ways human services contributes to the extraordinary time demands of a job is to have people sign "exempt" employment contracts.

Exempt status meant my job was not confined to a forty-hour workweek. Exempt status meant I could work seventy or more hours per week and not be paid any additional money. When I first signed an exempt contract, I remember thinking, "Oh, this is for those couple of weeks a year when I need to work extra." Heck no! Under an exempt boundary-free employment contract, I found it impossible to figure out where my days and weeks started and ended. There were no limits.

I rarely worked anything less than a sixty-hour week, and when I wasn't at work, I was on call. For seven years, in addition to my fifty-plus hour workweek, I was on call around the clock 24-7. One of the bigger boundaries I gradually defined was to stop signing exempt employment contracts. This personal decision helped me define my time and relieved me from feeling obligated to always be working. My hope is that you realize much sooner than I did that you do not have to endure the lack of boundaries endemic to the field of healthcare and human services.

You too will experience these boundary challenges and boundary conflicts. While some organizations manage time boundaries better than others, the truth is that you are the only person who can manage your boundaries. In fact, if you manage your boundaries, you will find yourself thriving in the many joys and benefits from having a meaningful career in healthcare and human services, making a difference, and feeling deeply connected to your colleagues over a lifetime. I eventually learned to manage every hour fiercely, and it has served me and my clients very well.

Defining your job

Boundaries—what you say yes to and what you say no to—come from the inside. They come from you. I know you think your employer manages your job description and, in most fields, that is true. Sometimes I read job postings in our sector and I want to cry. So many job descriptions have no boundaries at all. In healthcare and human services, no one will tell you this, but the best way to prevent becoming overwhelmed is defining your job.

Your job description is an important way for you to begin managing your boundaries and your time. Read your job description to see if it has clear, well-defined boundaries. Does the time allotted to do the job you're being asked to do make sense? You may find it is not possible to do your job within the hours of the day. Check your job description for a sprawling never-ending, demanding, unreasonable list of expectations. I can spot sprawl right away—I look for how many skills it takes to do the job as written.

Then ask yourself if your job description matches what you do. You may find yourself doing many things that are outside of your actual job description and that overload you with too much to do. Mira's job with triple the caseload, supervision, and extra tasks were all outside of her job description.

I recently read a job description that was titled volunteer manager. As I read the description, it included: cleaning the entire office building, accounting for the organization, payroll, board secretary, social media for the organization, answering phones for the organization, secretary to the executive director, calendar management for three administrators, writing a policy and procedure manual for the organization, event planning, attending meetings as needed, and volunteer training and placement. The office building cleaning, accounting and payroll, secretary work, and policy manual, were indications of sprawl. I thought board secretary was a bit of a stretch as well, but I could see how the organization might think of their board as volunteers and sneak those duties under the volunteer manager job description. But really, this was a job description that couldn't possibly be done in a forty-hour work week.

Only you can manage the boundaries of your job description in healthcare and human services. If you apply to jobs at different organizations, you will discover that there are differences in job descriptions. Hone in on the expectations of your job. Clarify and set boundaries around the job descriptions you sign up to do before you sign a contract. It is difficult to negotiate an improved job description after you have been consumed, exhausted, and drained by a sprawling job.

You may find yourself labeled as burned out and blamed for not doing enough self-care outside of work. But the reality is that the job is depleting you and self-care outside of work isn't going to fix the problem. Self-care around your job description is the solution. If you can't fix the job description, it is time to look for a job where you can work within set hours and have a doable job.

Healthcare and human service organizations can be needy organizations. The very same organization that wants you to be compassionate and resilient at all times, may be draining you with organization neediness. But despite what your job description says, you will be asked to do more. There is a sense of pride in our field for taking on more, but while you are gaining praise and recognition for doing extra work, you are on the stairway to overwhelm.

Taking time to understand your feelings will help you recognize your limits.

How you handle requests to do more than your actual job will be an ongoing issue. Up close or in the moment, you may think it is a temporary task that you are asked or required to do. However, you will be asked to do more countless times. There is nothing special about these requests, but notice how often you are offered to be paid more for the extra. The extra assignments can also lead to resentment and burnout.

These are opportunities for you to determine and set your boundaries and limits. Only you will know if you are feeling overloaded. Only you can protect your own resiliency by staying within your limits.

<u>Defining your role</u>

In addition to boundaries needed to prevent you from being overwhelmed with responsibilities, and managing your time; you also must look closely at boundaries with your clients. You will find the size of your caseload, the number of people you see in a day or in a week, makes a big difference in terms of how you feel. I think of boundaries and clients in two ways: the number of people I am working with at one time, and the invisible line between me and my clients. There is also the line between the hearts, an emotional connection and emotional boundary, and this line can be the hardest one to find.

If you work directly with clients, you have feelings when a client is suffering. Your culture and your own history may also influence how you deal with suffering, trauma, and distress. When you see suffering, you may feel there is more you can do to help. You have a strong sense of responsibility to others. You may become confused by your supportive care for a client and take responsibility for being their sole support system. I have seen this happen to very experienced practitioners.

Interestingly, in our field, supervisors watch newer staff and client boundaries closely, but it is the most experienced staff who I have seen step over boundaries with clients. People who have had lots of experience working with trauma will sometimes step over their boundary. Inexperienced people are actually not as vulnerable to this as the more experienced staff. I have seen it many times with experienced people. My guess is that less experienced staff don't feel capable of filling the voids they see and may be able to stay within boundaries. Experienced practitioners, on the other hand, can act as if boundaries are somehow beneath them or only for novices.

You may find that instead of helping a client connect to resources, you offer to be their sole resource, to do more than your job. You will cope with this by saying, "It is just temporary" or "Just this once." At the exact moment when you are going beyond the bounds of your practice, trying to help someone, you are at high risk and a danger to yourself. By way of example, there was a caseworker who believed a client needed a place to stay and took the client home. He gave the client a warm, safe bed in his own house. The caseworker believed the client needed help leaving a domestic violence situation. The client then stole jewelry, returned to her abusive partner, filed a professional misconduct complaint against the caseworker, and later a lawsuit for damages, accusing the caseworker of making sexual advances.

Your clients are not your personal friends. You may think a client has no friends or resources, and you may feel you must fill that void in a person's life. But if you see a void in relationships around a client, you can encourage them to attend support groups and build relationships. You cannot fill that friendship need.

We are always vulnerable to feeling that we must step in closer to help. Witnessing suffering and overwhelm is a very vulnerable place for compassionate healthcare and human service workers. This is the pain point for our field. There will be needs you can't fill. There will be resources that the client can't access. The waitlist may be long. The suffering may not be something you can prevent.

This is why it is so important to have supervisors, mentors, and colleagues to talk about how you are feeling, how you are struggling with seeing terrible suffering, and how you feel powerless to change the situation. You need their help to accept that you are not superhuman. It was my mentors who helped me navigate when the headwinds blew, helping me to work smarter to get what was needed for those I served.

Notes:

_____

_____

_____

_____

_____

_____

_____

_____

_____

_____

_____

_____

_____

_____

_____

_____

_____

CHAPTER SEVEN:

Healthy Supports for the Helpers

One way to help you stay within boundaries is to have frequent, ongoing boundary discussions. Questions, conversations, and thoughtful examination of boundaries is critical for those working in healthcare and human services. Our field places so much pressure on our boundaries and limited resources, so discussions with the intention of clarifying boundaries can be quite useful. You will experience boundary murkiness, boundary conflicts, and boundary changes. Boundary conversations are rare, but if those conversations are more frequent, they can help build resiliency for everyone who delivers services in our field.

A second way to help build stronger boundaries is to create an advocacy effort or join an existing effort to work for needed changes and to address the needs you are seeing. Advocacy can take a long time to yield results, but it is an outlet for the truth. It is a way for your work to benefit more than one person, and it is a way to address the strong feelings you may have about what you are witnessing.

Training is a third way to enable you to help yourself. Both trauma training and boundary development training can make a big difference. Trauma exposure affects your boundaries. Trauma training may be more accessible to you, but boundary training and development is an ongoing process. Please look into the books and classes I have developed on boundary development to help you build and maintain your boundaries.

A fourth way to help yourself is to care for you outside of work. Taking great care of you is essential if you are going to feel happy and fulfilled working with other people all the time. Look closely at your personal relationships. Are you in loving supportive relationships? If you struggle with boundaries in your personal life, it will wear you down. Taking time to connect with friends, rest, play, practice your passions, and feed your soul are all essential to supporting your boundaries and your resiliency.

Take time to reflect:

- Read your job description. Now write your actual job description. List everything that you do. Does it seem reasonable or doable for the number of hours you work? Are there some changes that need to be discussed with your supervisor about your job, the hours you work, and the tasks you are doing?

- Would you benefit from trauma training and boundary development training, and self-care training? Discuss with your supervisor training you need to support your resiliency.

- What do you do outside of work to take care of you, support your resiliency, and feed your soul daily? What do you need to add?

Notes:

_____

_____

_____

_____

_____

_____

_____

_____

_____

_____

_____

_____

_____

_____

_____

PART III:

Widespread Overwhelm, the Overwhelm Around You

Notes:

_____

_____

_____

_____

_____

_____

_____

_____

_____

_____

_____

_____

_____

_____

_____

_____

CHAPTER EIGHT:

What is Community Overwhelm

Story about Manny

Manny is working in the local hospital as the director of communications. It is a small hospital serving a rural community. He lives in the local community; in fact, he grew up there. His family has settled in the area along with other immigrants. All of them are from the same war-torn country.

Manny loves his job at the local hospital. Every day, people he knows are served in the hospital, people who are neighbors, friends, firefighters, teachers, and parents of friends. He believes the hospital provides great care to his community. Then, a series of events happens that shakes Manny and his faith in everything he trusts.

The hospital is struggling with the recent news that an audit shows money was missing from the hospital accounts. The hospital administrator has left town in the middle of the night. The community is outraged at the hospital board and wants answers. There is fear and rumors that the hospital will be closed.

A week later, there is an explosion at the local high school science lab. Three students are killed, and twenty others have severe burns. The hospital is instantly full of parents, school teachers, students, reporters, and television crews. Manny feels solely responsible for getting information to those who need it.

He is overwhelmed emotionally by the loss of lives and injuries. Children need to be identified, and parents need help. The hospital needs to call in extra medical staff. Air transport needs to be arranged for some of the children to get to other hospitals.

Manny feels helpless; he wanted to save those kids. He doesn't want to talk to the reporters, and he is angry that they are crowding the hospital. The other hospital administrators have so much to arrange. He feels alone in the sea of people swarming the hospital.

He decides to clear the building of television crews and people not directly injured. He announces parents and immediate family only are permitted to stay and everyone else has to go. Rather than being supportive and helpful, teachers and reporters rage at him. Manny is struggling, too. As tears stream down his face, he tries to help parents get the information they need.

The hospital is in chaos. The person charged with leading the hospital has left in disgrace a week prior. Staff in the hospital are busy taking care of the injured children. Suspicion and questions come from the families as they wonder why their child are not being airlifted first. The community of immigrants wonders who they can trust. Are the white children getting served first? Who decides who is to be treated and when? There is even suspicion that the hospital somehow caused the explosion in the science lab to show how important their hospital services are.

Manny is horrified by the suspicion and rumors. As he looks back on the day, he cries as he talks of feeling that he has failed everyone who needs him. Manny feels it personally because he is part of the community, and the overwhelm is community-wide.

Think about this situation:

- When have you been in a community that was overwhelmed?

- How did it affect you personally?

- How long was the community recovery process and what was involved for healthcare and human service workers?

Defining community overwhelm

The earlier parts of this book were dedicated to recognizing and supporting one person who is overwhelmed. In Part One, we looked at clients, and in Part Two, we looked at healthcare and human service staff. Overwhelm can also be widespread across a community or many communities.

Community overwhelm is shared and felt by many people at the same time. When there are permanent and irreplaceable losses, the community in some ways will be changed. It may be a traumatic event or a series of events. Local healthcare and human service resources may be inundated and possibly unable to meet all the needs of those harmed.

An example of this occurred in 2008–2010 as the recession hit individuals, homeowners, businesses, banks, and contractors around the world. In my thirty years in practice, I have never seen anything like the 2008 recession. In healthcare and human services, we were treating everyone for stress-related illness, trauma, depression, and anxiety. In addition to losing their jobs, people lost their health insurance, their homes and, for some, they lost their families as marriages crumbled under the pressure. People got cancer, had heart attacks, and lost their life savings, all at once.

In a 2009 report by University of Albany sociologist Kate W. Strully in the journal *Demography*,[17] "Strully found that losing a job when a business closes increased the odds of fair or poor health by 54 percent among workers with no preexisting health conditions, and increased by 83 percent the odds of new health conditions likely triggered by job loss—stress-related conditions such as stroke, hypertension, heart disease, arthritis, diabetes, and emotional and psychiatric problems."

There was nothing usual or typical about treating people who had their lives turned upside down in the recession. Many did not recover, and many communities continue to struggle. Agencies providing healthcare and human services had disaster plans in place for earthquakes, power outages, and other events, but our systems were not prepared for massive unemployment, homelessness, and widespread loss of health insurance coverage.

When you are working in a community that has been suddenly overwhelmed, coordination between healthcare and human resources can be very demanding. Pressures mount as healthcare and human resource workers are expected to coordinate services to fill gaps and reduce waiting times for clients. Your job requires that you be resilient and

17 Kate W. Strully, "Job Loss and Health in the U.S. Labor Market," Demography, Vol. 46, No. 2 (May 2009): 221-246.

compassionate no matter what is happening. Finding recovery time for workers, ensuring all workers are getting their own basic needs met is essential when a community is overwhelmed. Helping the helpers is essential.

Yet, what I saw during the recession was helpers treating others while little or no attention was given to the helpers themselves. Health and human service workers had the same tragic losses unfolding in their own families. It was not possible for the healthcare and human service workers to be exempt from the community overwhelm. Sharing our communal grief during the recession was a way we could acknowledge and support each other. Providers of healthcare and human services relied on a communal togetherness to help us manage together through it.

When it comes to community overwhelm, we are experiencing the overwhelm with our clients.

Community overwhelm may not be limited to a single event or trigger. A community may be overwhelmed by a series of incidents or an ongoing struggle with unsolved problems that result in a chronic state of overwhelm. It may be a problem that has historic roots, and continues to impact and devastate the people of the community. There also may be strong denial by the dominant culture that the community is overwhelmed.

Your community may be denied the appropriate support and assistance, leaving healthcare and human service providers, and educators alone on the frontlines to care for people without adequate resources.

Some examples that have overwhelmed communities include: water pollution, AIDS, Zika virus, shootings, unemployment, methamphetamine, and racism. Healthcare and human services see these issues every day. But when you see them widespread in a community, it can be difficult to create hope. Hope is one of the main medicines we have. While we treat the people who are impacted and devastated, what do we offer the helpers to maintain their own sense of hope?

Is working in an overwhelmed community the best fit for you

In the face of community overwhelm, it may feel selfish or ridiculous to stop and care for yourself. The devastation around you can dwarf any of your basic needs. Do not be judgmental with yourself. Not everyone can or should work in chronic overwhelm. It can damage your resiliency if you are overwhelmed working in chronic community overwhelm. To sustain in the tough conditions, it helps if you are wired for optimism. Research has shown that you are either wired this way or not.

In a 2013 article, David Hecht of the Institute of Cognitive Neuroscience, found that:

"[O]ptimism and pessimism are differentially associated with the two cerebral hemispheres. High self-esteem, a cheerful attitude that tends to look at the positive aspects of a given situation, as well as an optimistic belief in a bright future are associated with physiological activity in the left-hemisphere (LH). In contrast, a gloomy viewpoint, an inclination to focus on the negative part and exaggerate its significance, low self-esteem as well as a pessimistic view on what the future holds are interlinked with neurophysiological processes in the right-hemisphere (RH)."[18]

He went on to state, "When attention to the positive and brighter side of life does not come naturally, it can still be achieved through a conscious and mindful effort, and this process involves the LH. Cognitive re-appraisal is often used in psychotherapy where a person is trained to change his/her point-of-view on negative events by focusing on the positive aspects."[19]

I am one of those people who are wired for optimism. But even with that, after years of working with teens who had been homeless and abused, I had to accept that I could no longer work with frontline children suffering from abuse. I reached a threshold inside where I could not tolerate the pain I felt around abused children. I had to accept this truth that I was emotionally too full from witnessing so much of it. I could work with adults who were reflecting on abuse and torture but not children.

You have to know where you are. The expectation you may feel inside is that you are equipped to serve everyone. It helps to learn where you are effective, where you can maintain

18 David Hecht, "The Neural Basis of Optimism and Pessimism,"
Exp. Neurobiol., 2013 Sep; 22(3): 173-199, https://www.ncbi.nlm.nih.gov/pmc/articles/PMC3807005/.
19Id.

resiliency, where you genuinely feel hope and optimism, and where you have the capacity to manage your own feelings and pain. You may find that you have a special gift with kids, or the elderly, or poverty, or people who are incarcerated, or those with mental health issues. Everyone has special gifts.

Where you feel hope and optimism is where you need to work.

Notes:

_____

_____

_____

_____

_____

_____

_____

_____

_____

_____

_____

_____

_____

_____

_____

CHAPTER NINE:

How Do You Treat Community Overwhelm

Earning trust in communities

When you work with a community, you earn the confidence of the community slowly. Trust is earned in community work. The hospital where Manny worked had lost the trust of the community. The suspicions and rumors were painful to Manny, who was committed to his community.

One way to establish your trust is to be compassionate about what is happening in a community. Kindness is extremely important in community work. When you are around people who are depleted, you will see some frustration dealing with feelings. People are short on patience, quick to make jokes, jokes that may not be funny and reveal cynicism and burnout. The jokes may actually make fun of those who are suffering. Bringing your compassion out may feel awkward. But your compassion can help remind people to be kind.

Trust begins by being predictable. Be consistent about what you do and be consistent about your boundaries. Your boundaries are how you run on time, show up when you say you will, and define what you can do. Show up and be consistent. Don't test the patience of overwhelmed clients in an overwhelmed community.

Be prepared to feed and water yourself. When I work in overwhelmed communities, I bring my own lunch, snacks, water, and whatever I will need. I come prepared to meet my own needs.

Be responsive to needs and help prioritize care. Communicate with other providers in the community when possible, get releases from clients, and do not violate privacy laws. Protecting the privacy of community members is another way you earn trust.

Dealing with community overwhelm is different when you live in the community you are serving. The heartache runs even deeper when you personally know those whose lives are affected. Not everyone can work where they live. Manny had loved working in his community, and when things were going well, it was easier for him to manage. You may find that living in a different community gives you a bit of a sanctuary for yourself. Or you may find that living where you work is meaningful to you.

The power of modeling

As a provider of healthcare and human service in an overwhelmed community, you become a model for the community. Your self-care is one way you offer hope. You are a model of strength, of healing, and a willingness to persevere side by side with the community. You may even be scarred or wounded by the things that have hurt the community, so you are able to say that you understand surviving and healing.

Being a model of hope in the face of community overwhelm is often born from your own life experience. If you came from poverty, there was addiction in your home, you were unemployed, you were a teen mother, if you recovered from addiction or depression, you are a phoenix that rose from the ashes. You have healed from something very hard. All your friends went to prison, but you did not. Your entire culture is plagued with alcoholism, but yet you don't drink. Your family was extremely poor, yet you became educated.

A place for you

Where can you safely feel your own devastation, your fear, your own overwhelm? Sometimes, behind closed doors is the only safe place for you to come apart. Taking care of yourself and honoring your true feelings is essential to manage what you are witnessing.

Everyone in healthcare and human services needs time for their own grief, to acknowledge the community you are part of, and all that you feel.

It can be draining on your mind and body when you are in a community that is overwhelmed. Every encounter, every client may be suffering so deeply, you aren't getting any sort of balance in your work. There aren't lighter issues. Working hour after hour requires so much from you to be present and to not ruminate on the person from the last hour while you are with your next client.

Our hearts may be barely equipped for witnessing all the suffering.

Dealing with community overwhelm takes practice, patience, and experience. It is similar to marathon running. You build the endurance and capacity to work with community overwhelm over time, gradually. You build your endurance with training and caring supervision. Supervisors need to be very attentive and available to newer staff as they gain experience working with community overwhelm.

Community overwhelm is not always predictable. It is best to prepare and train newer staff with trauma training and boundary development in advance of anything happening. Many times when a community event hits, frontline people in healthcare and human services are engaging in the issue for the very first time. If staff are newer to community work, it helps if they are provided supervision to learn and process as they serve. It doesn't help when supervisors are pulled to the frontline to help as many people as possible and their staff lose necessary back-up and support. Supervisors need to be mindful and stay engaged with their staff.

Finding community for you

It can be challenging to find ways to participate in community for fun, not in your work role but as a person. When you find places where you want to belong, you may need to figure out how to maintain boundaries to give yourself a break from processing and helping. You know things about people and have insight. People may turn to you and start talking about something very private and ask you for advice about a life challenge. Recognize where you are and why you are there and allow yourself to have some boundaries.

For example, I love knitting. If I join a knitting group or class, I am there to knit and talk about knitting. I try to leave my role as a therapist and join in as a knitter. If someone approaches me for therapeutic support or wants to step aside and update me on a situation in their life, I will say, "This sounds important. Give me a call later and we can talk then." Later for me means, I will return the call during my workday.

Take time to reflect:

- What experiences do you have in community overwhelm? What have you learned from those experiences?

- How did you do with your self-care during community overwhelm? Did you feel guilty? Were you able to model self-care? What was challenging about that?

- Where is your safe place to express your feelings?

Notes:

_____

_____

_____

_____

_____

_____

_____

_____

_____

_____

CHAPTER TEN:

What is Organization Overwhelm

Defining organization overwhelm

I was sitting at a long table, waiting for the seven other board members to walk in for our second board meeting. As the board members made their way to their seats, I could feel a heaviness, a load each was carrying. Slowly, the room began to fill with tired people who worked hard all day at big jobs and then came to volunteer on a board. I had taken time to carefully review the finances of this organization, and there was no escaping the fact that it was financially in a hole.

When an organization is overwhelmed,
the signs of it are everywhere.

I had spent time meeting with each board member and could only conclude that this was the hardest working group of volunteers I had ever met. The programs offered by the organization were useful, meaningful, and necessary. So, I wondered, why was the organization running in the red, and why was everyone on the board exhausted?

They hired me to be their executive director. There was plenty for me to do, but my instinct told me that the most important thing I could do was take the organization out of a state of overwhelm. To lift the load off the overworked board, I needed to expand the number of people working behind the scenes. I could have picked any number of starting points for my work with the organization, but I prioritized treating the overwhelm first.

I had learned through experience that overwhelmed organizations lose talent and have trouble with priorities. The loss of talent and the muddled priorities create a continuous string of distracting problems. Best to fix the overwhelm first and help the organization get stronger from the inside. Stress affects how the organization functions, how it feels to work around staff and volunteers, and how often the decisions made actually makes the overwhelm worse. Overwhelmed organizations can have symptoms similar to those of an overwhelmed person.

Recognizing if you work in an overwhelmed organization

When you work in an overwhelmed organization, it can feel as if you are personally failing all the time.

You wonder what are you doing wrong if you can't get your work done.

You believe you must take work home at night, even if you don't get paid for those hours.

You feel like leadership or management is not listening.

You feel like you are failing when things fall through the cracks.

You get angry that your coworkers seem nonresponsive when you send a request.

You are stunned that inappropriate behavior from a coworker is tolerated or ignored rather than dealt with.

Your feel like all managers above you are too busy to meet with you when you have a question.

You worry about your clients and about seeing their complaints go unaddressed.

You feel like everyone around you is too busy to help you with a task.

You are unappreciated for your effort.

You hear rumors about impending doom or questions about how much longer the organization or its programs will continue to operate.

You feel like the leaders around you aren't competent to manage or lead.

You can't figure out the priorities for your job.

You notice that certain positions are hard to fill.

When you are experiencing all of this at your job, you may think it is you. But all of these are the signs of an overwhelmed organization.

The impact on you

Pay attention to the impact the organization is having on you. You may feel incompetent, sick, stressed, and defeated by your job. In addition, you may be surrounded by highly stressed coworkers. There are many different types of settings for healthcare and human services. It is okay to try out large versus small; private versus public; a national organization versus grassroots versus government run. You never know what it will feel like to work in a particular organization. It is helpful to try different types and different sizes to find a good fit for you. The key is to find a place to work where you feel healthy.

Notes:

_____

_____

_____

_____

_____

_____

CHAPTER ELEVEN:

How Do You Treat Organization Overwhelm

Five steps leaders and managers can take to help an overwhelmed organization

If you are a new leader or manager in an organization, there are some immediate things you can do to turn around an overwhelmed organization. That nonprofit that was in a financial hole and had an exhausted board needed some new energized people added to the board. I did not get rid of the tired hardworking people. Instead, I brought in additional people to carry the load. In two years, we had the organization back in fiscal health and a board that had increased from seven people to twenty-one!

Of course, each organization is different. But there are some common issues that can be used as starting points in any overwhelmed organization. If you are a new manager, you may not have ever seen an organization turn around. But most organizations can recover from overwhelm.

The first step is to identify what is overwhelming the organization. Listen to staff and learn about what is overwhelming them. Always with overwhelm, listen first. Listen and acknowledge that things are, in fact, overwhelming.

The next step is to get help prioritizing what you do and what staff are doing. Use facilitators to help prioritize. It can be a difficult process to select priorities when everything seems important. I would start with one or two things that seem doable. It will give your team tremendous confidence to achieve the one or two things, to have focus, and accomplish something by prioritizing.

The third step is to reduce the load. Review job descriptions. In the most general way, overwhelm always has something to do with the load and people being spread too thin with too much to do. Managers need to reduce the load. Having employees work while overwhelmed results in poor thinking, poor problem solving, and a weakening of the overall effectiveness of the organization. Address capacity issues: Are you short staffed? Is it too difficult to recruit and keep talent? How can reductions in load allow people to focus on the priorities?

A fourth step is to streamline communication. Reduce and shorten the e-mails and memos sent throughout the organization. Stop overwhelming your team with too much information, too much to wade through, and too many tasks.

The fifth goal is to improve and shorten meetings. It helps to adopt a set of standards and meeting protocols for your team. If long meetings are needed, it is important they be facilitated by people who are trained in meeting facilitation.

It takes a tremendous effort to have employees commit to supporting an organization that is recovering from overwhelm. You need to think about your personal capacity to lead or manage in an overwhelmed organization. This is not a good fit for every person. You need to think about the energy required and the commitment to stay invested in a process of fixing something that isn't working.

Creating healthy workplaces

You have a role in creating a healthy work environment. When you take care of yourself,—stopping for lunch, taking time to connect to people around you, discussing priorities, and managing your boundaries—you are protecting yourself from overwhelm and modeling for others around you how to do the same.

Some of the smallest of things can create a big impact in having a healthy team and healthy organization. You can take a lunch break. You can say, "Let's choose priorities." You can be a leader in this way. The impact you will have on those around you will make a difference, and I encourage you to support your own healthy behavior and challenge yourself to take it further.

I believe in organization resiliency. It comes from having boundaries, healthy ways of operating, listening to staff and clients, providing quality supervision, forging valuable partnerships, and committing to not overwhelm staff. As Diane Coutu so eloquently explains in her luminous journal article "How Resilience Works," "Resilient people…possess three characteristics: a staunch acceptance of reality; a deep belief, often buttressed by strongly held values, that life is meaningful;

and an uncanny ability to improvise. You can bounce back from hardship with just one or two of these qualities, but you will only be truly resilient with all three. These three characteristics hold true for resilient organizations as well."[20] She goes on to state that, "Resilient people and companies face reality with staunchness, make meaning of hardship instead of crying out in despair, and improvise solutions from thin air. Others do not."[21]

Organizations can recover from being overwhelmed. They can't recover by themselves. You will be part of making things better. It can be incredibly satisfying to see organizations built to do meaningful useful work operating in healthy ways. This kind of recovery will earn the organization a great reputation in the community, and their strength will keep building with a positive energy.

20 Diane Coutu, "How Resilience Works," Harvard Business Review (May 2002 Issue), https://hbr.org/2002/05/how-resilience-works
21 Id.

Put into practice:

- Look at the organization where you work or attend school. What signs of overwhelm do you notice in your organization?

- How is the overwhelm affecting you? What are you willing to do to support yourself to recover?

- What healthy thing can you be known for and share with coworkers?

- Do you have a knack for partnering with others and sharing ideas to improve things where you work? Is there a way to share those ideas and get support to implement them? If you are in an organization that is not interested, can you move to an organization that finds your ideas energizing and will support you to try ideas?

Leadership

A few years ago, I was coaching someone who was a first time executive director of a nonprofit organization. When we met, I asked her to bring all of her observations about the organization. She had an impressive list, and I knew she had a big job in front of her to clean up the organization's mess.

At one point, she looked at me exasperated and said, "There are goddam beetles in the walls of the building. I have to deal with beetles!"

I nodded.

She said, "I don't want to deal with beetles. I want to lay out a bright vision. I have ideas. I want to move forward with new things."

I assured her there would be a time in the future when she would get a chance to bring her vision and ideas forward. But at the moment, the organization needed a leader who could tackle beetles and every other mess that was overwhelming the organization. Inside, I was deeply impressed with her; the list she had made showed her keen awareness of the issues. I knew I was standing in front of a leader who could tackle the overwhelm and clean up the mess.

She asked me how long I thought it would take for her to clean up everything that was overwhelming the organization. I told her the truth: three years if she stayed focused. She asked why it would take so long. I looked at her list of observations and thought about the team she would need to help her. I told her that the effort would involve more than just her—that she would need to engage a team.

It did take her a while, but she used the support she got when she hired a coach. She built her team, and she tackled all the beetles—the ones in the wall and the ones in the organization. Then, she embarked with her team on her bright bold vision.

Handling overwhelm is the job of every leader

Leaders have a significant and close relationship to overwhelm. I taught leadership development for seven years. The topic of overwhelm was sorely missing from books and discussions about leadership. I came to believe that overwhelm was the elephant in the room—everyone knew it was there. Leaders I worked with used the word over and over, but no one addressed it directly. As I talked about this book while I was writing it, one leader said, "Are there any leaders who aren't overwhelmed?" This is a profound question worth asking ourselves.

Leaders are facing a very big job. They have to prevent or tackle their own overwhelm, their organization overwhelm, staff overwhelm, and community overwhelm, and ensure their organizations have the capacity to care for clients who are overwhelmed.

Growing Leaders

Leaders grow leaders. Your leadership development begins the day you start working in our field. Be selective about the kind of leaders surrounding you. This may not be very obvious when you start a job, but if you realize you do not like the kind of leaders you are around, you have a very good reason to leave a position. Place yourself around other leaders whom you admire, people who have experience in our field, handle stress well, have time to mentor, and who invest time in getting to know you.

The longer I worked in our field, the more I realized the importance of protecting myself by surrounding myself only with great leaders. Since I was an executive director, I was careful about the leaders surrounding me on the board of directors and on the staff. I wasn't looking to be surrounded by people who agreed with me. I wanted to be surrounded by people I admired and who had the time to help me build strong, capable staff and a strong organization truly able to serve the community.

You need to take time and be honest with yourself about finding the right setting and surrounding yourself with the right leaders so you can thrive and develop your abilities. It doesn't help if you work in an overwhelmed environment and are not supervised, nurtured, or given support to become a great leader. As a leader in this field, you must pay an enormous amount of attention to important issues, such as finding cures for illness, solving homelessness, and stopping child abuse. You understand your mission, your purpose, and your why. There is a delicate balance between the often painful issues you are addressing and the ways you support your staff to maintain their health while doing this work. While we are in the business of doing meaningful work, we must not overlook the external stress and the internal distress we are subject to when doing this work.

As a leader, it is your job to know what is overwhelming your staff and the organization.

Staff members can only do so much to address overwhelm. If leaders are creating overwhelm, staff will not be able to stop it. While everyone can play a part in preventing or cleaning up overwhelm, ultimately it is a leadership responsibility to keep the organization out of a state of overwhelm.

As a leader, you start with you. Get yourself out of a state of overwhelm before you try tackling the organization. You need to increase your own self-care and well-being, select priorities, recover, and rest to restore your mind. Practice on you. As you see gains and feel better, you will know when you are ready to support your staff and organization to do the same. Some of the staff will start changing merely because they see you establishing boundaries and doing better self-care. As a leader, you will notice that others start doing what they see you doing. But this won't happen for all staff. They won't just "catch it" from you. You will need to be intentional about reaching out to your staff. Some will be more deeply entrenched in the overwhelm. You will need to support your staff as they identify boundaries and grow their self-care skills.

Dealing with Change

One of the vulnerable spots for overwhelm is during large changes in an organization. Change is no longer an event that happens every few years. Instead, change has become a constant in the healthcare sector. Change is happening all the time.

Some organizations are responding to the constant change by training staff to be more resilient in the face of change. It is not the change itself or the process that is the issue, rather it is the personal resiliency of staff. Staff who may be drained, depleted, and overworked are then told they aren't being resilient or compassionate enough.

Leaders must be careful not to blame staff for burnout.

It is not useful to blame overwhelmed staff or make them responsible for the depletion being caused by overload. It is better to be honest about the overload and to identify how administration is going to intervene to stop the overload and manage the changes in a way to make them less overwhelming. It takes listening and problem solving together—administrators and staff—to make the change without creating overwhelm on staff and clients. Remember, those of us who work in health and human services are not personally more abundant in resilience than other people. We are all vulnerable to overwhelm.

Your self-care is crucial to your leadership development.

Leaders are grown. You are not alone in a silo. You are in a sector, a field that needs you, working with clients who need you. Our field needs you to lead. You need to have sharpened attention, strategic thinking, and problem-solving that are core to working in healthcare and human services. You need to protect your mind and your compassion.

If you become overwhelmed, it will affect your problem-solving abilities. It is your job to protect yourself from overwhelm. Your ability to do this is not solely based on how much balance you have in your private life. It also comes from looking closely at the work you are doing, what you are expecting of yourself, and how reasonable and supportive your team is.

Leadership, great leadership, is what we can pass on to each other in this field. If you experience it, you will be able to provide it to others. It is essential that you surround yourself with people you consider great leaders. Managing overwhelm is not easy, but we can't underestimate the power and influence of great leaders to make things less overwhelming. Some days, you are dealing with beetles in the walls. Everyday there are things competing for a leaders' attention. Great leaders handle a wide range of things while not allowing the beetles in the wall to bring the house down.

Take time to reflect:

- How do you feel about the current leaders surrounding you? What observations do you have about the leaders surrounding you?

- How are you doing with your own self-care and preventing your own overwhelm?

- Where are you a leader and in what ways can you prevent overwhelm?

CHAPTER TWELVE:

Create a Sanctuary and Be a Sanctuary for Others

I was having dinner with a friend at her house. She prepared a special meal of my favorite foods. It was my birthday. I arrived at her house a bit disoriented. I had seen a client earlier in the day whose suffering was very much on my mind. I was lost in my head and heart. I wasn't talking about the client. I was trying to be present at the birthday dinner, taste the food, and ask my friend for a story about her recent trip to Paris. I think I heard a third of what my friend was saying. The pain I felt inside for my client earlier in the day had overtaken my mind.

My friend saw right through my charade of trying to be present. She reached across the table, touched my hand softly, and asked, "How do you do this work all the time? How do you handle hearing hard stories?" She is a human resources director, and I know she hears hard stories often, too. I thought for a minute. She knew right where I was inside. But her question struck me, shook me, and reminded me that some days are full of very hard things.

How do we do this work? It was a great question. I went upstairs in my head and asked myself, "Well, how do I do this?" And then I knew my answer.

"When I am working with someone who is suffering, I remember all the people I have seen heal. I know they will heal. I know for you and me, our job is to bring hope and caring."

Bringing hope and caring

This is what I do, and this is what you do: We bring the hope and caring. In the days ahead, there will be times when you may feel overwhelmed. When you are overwhelmed, it is you who needs the hope and caring that you generously give to others.

Anyone on the frontlines in healthcare needs to be compassionate with themselves. You are not an unlimited being. I am not an unlimited being. You do not have more strength than other beings. You do not have a special shield to deflect all of the pain you witness. I don't have a magic wand to deflect all the pain either. You are human.

---

*You have emotions to tend to in your own life
and your own garden, all the time.*

When you help others with their lives and their struggles, you have entered into their garden. Your work may bring you into many other people's gardens all through the day. You need a way to bring yourself home. Your home—yourself—needs to be a place of love, kindness, and compassion.

I understand when I am tired and need a rest. I have finally learned how to rest. My medical file no longer says, "exhausted." I understand if I can't listen. My ears can be full. It is okay for me to do something visual and give my ears a rest. It's okay for me to nurture myself and take good care of me. I don't feel guilty about it.

I learned that I must dwell in the compassion I offer to others.

Create a sanctuary for yourself

The place where you dwell inside, must become a sanctuary. You need a place to compassionately care for yourself. Your sanctuary needs to be emotionally safe. Your sanctuary can be anywhere. It can be in a journal, your car, your bathtub, the forest, or the back porch at night. As long as you are there, a sanctuary can be anywhere. It is a place where you offer some care and nurturance to you.

I have a practice that I do in my head to help me recognize when I am being judgmental, critical, or demanding of myself. I ask myself, "How is this thought or belief making me feel? Is it putting more pressure on me? Do I need more pressure?"

These questions free me. No, I do not need more pressure. I have noticed that my compassion expands with this practice for others and for myself. If you need to work on your judgment of yourself or pressure on yourself, please look at Byron Katie's website and book.[22] She teaches people how to use self-inquiry to free yourself from useless, restricting, thoughts. Her methods are simple and easy to learn. She has four questions to use with yourself on her website.

---

22 [Byron Katie, Who Would You Be Without Your Story (Carlsbad: Hay House, 2008; www.thework.com]

In addition to a sanctuary, you will need a practice to keep your heart open. I highly recommend that you routinely take courses that help you nurture compassion and self-care. There are courses and books offering many lessons on compassion. These practices will help sustain you and carry you over troubled waters. If you don't have a practice to help you with compassion, you will need one. In healthcare, it is essential.

If you do not feel compassion or have lost your sense of feeling, you will be less effective in guiding a person towards caring enough about themselves to help themselves. A compassionate practice is like a stress reduction practice. People want to learn how to reduce their stress when they are at the peak of stress. If you never do stress reduction, it is less beneficial when you start at a time when you are suffering from massive stress. It is more effective to have a stress reduction set of practices that you do daily. Then, when something very stressful happens, you have the practice to help you effectively lower your stress. Compassion is similar to stress reduction. You need to stay connected to your heart center.

When I am in the therapy room with people, I want to be sure that my clients can feel an energy from my heart and mind that is calm, soothing, and supportive. In order for my clients to feel this from me, I need to be this. When you are with your clients, they deserve compassionate care. You may not feel compassion for everyone. You may not feel hope in every situation. Notice where you draw the line. Notice where your compassion ends, or where your hope and caring may run dry.

We need to examine the boundaries of our compassion. We need to recognize and respect our limits. When you find the boundary of your compassion or hopefulness for your clients, it is important to change the population you are working with and find the right mix.

Even if you are at the very start of your career and haven't seen enough healing to count on it, you can count on the fact that you can bring hope and caring to every client. I want you to know that your ability to share hope and caring with your client will help them through the largest of life's difficulties. But you must be careful that you stay within the boundaries of healthy practices and not go so overboard with caring for your clients that you are no longer living in your own life. If I am not careful, I could be on the phone or responding to e-mails at all hours. I need to have limits about when I am working with clients and when I am not.

As I think about the immediate future for healthcare and human services, the days that are right in front of us, I am aware that you will be facing many unknowns. New challenges may feel quite overwhelming. You will be seeing many changes. In the days ahead, I want you to know the things that make a difference, the skills of hope and caring, your ability to define boundaries, your perseverance and leadership; those will stand the test of time.

May you dwell in the compassion that you offer to others.

Take time to reflect:

- Think about some of the ways you are hard on yourself. Write down a short list of the things that come to mind. Pick one thing on your list to practice bringing your compassion, hope, and caring.

- What could you do to be supportive rather than hard on yourself?

- Describe the ideal sanctuary for you. What could you do in your real life to create your sanctuary?

- Do some research on authors who write about compassion. Find some ideas that inspire you from one of the authors. Carry their words in your pocket to read when you need.

- Are you doing the things that bring you joy? What is the next thing you can say "yes" to that will bring you joy?

Notes:

**Use this 10% off discount code and join me in
the eCourses designed to accompany this book.**

10% off discount code:

sarri-gilman-1706

You can find the eCourses on my website
www.sarrigilman.com

I worked with a wonderful team from the Foundation for
Healthy Generations to create these eCourses to deepen your
self-care and boundary skills in a fun online format.

Made in the USA
Lexington, KY
24 June 2017